The Art and Science of Raising Your Autistic Child

A Holistic Approach to Manage Meltdowns, Improve Social Skills, and Support Neurodiverse Family Dynamics

K.M. Burnham

Contents

For my daughters.

Thank you for gifting me your wisdom, perspectives, laughter, and, most importantly, the opportunity to be your mom.

A Note on Language and Identity

In the journey of writing this book and in my personal experience raising two autistic daughters, I have given considerable thought to the language used to discuss autism and identity.

A significant choice was the use of identity-first language (IFL)—saying "autistic child" instead of "child with autism." This decision was not made lightly, but it is grounded in a deep respect for the preferences expressed by many in the autistic community. Identity-first language emphasizes that being autistic is an integral part of a person's identity, much like cultural and gender identities. It acknowledges autism not as a condition to be kept at arm's length but as a vital component of who a person is. This perspective aligns with the strengths-based approach of this book, which views autism as a difference rather than a deficit. This choice also reflects the broader shift within the autistic community and among neurodiversity advocates toward embracing and owning one's neurotype.

However, it's important to note that language preferences can vary widely among individuals. Some may prefer person-first language (PFL), which emphasizes the individual before the diagnosis, as in "child with autism." This preference is equally valid and deserves respect.

The decision to use identity-first language in this book also stems from my interactions and personal discussions with many autistic individuals and their families who express a strong preference for IFL, finding it more affirming of their identity. This choice supports the narrative of acceptance and pride in one's neurodivergent identity.

However, it's crucial to recognize and honor each person's self-identification. Because of this, I advocate asking individuals about their language preferences in conversations and interactions. This respectful practice acknowledges the personal nature of identity and affirms each person's autonomy to define themselves.

Through this book, I aim to share strategies and insights that contribute to a culture of respect, understanding, and affirmation of all aspects of autistic identity. By choosing identity-first language, I hope to reflect the voices and preferences of many in the autistic community and encourage ongoing dialogue about the power of language in shaping our perceptions and experiences.

Introduction

The day I understood my youngest daughter's attempt to ask for "a glass of water" might seem ordinary to some, but for us, it was nothing short of miraculous. In that brief moment, our world, often so full of confusion, frustration, and relentless worrying, paused. It was a breakthrough that highlighted both the immense challenges and profound joys of raising autistic children. The heart of this book beats from these personal victories and trials.

I am a mother, first and foremost, to two incredible autistic daughters, one diagnosed in childhood, the other as an adult. However, my journey through the landscapes of autism is not just personal; it is professional. In my personal life, I've immersed myself in learning and applying various therapeutic approaches, driven by my deep desire to provide the best support for my girls. In my professional life, I helped establish a program of sensory-friendly theater offerings for autistic children at my performance venue, working directly with the autistic community. This dual perspective as a parent and a professional has equipped me with insights and strategies I am eager to share with you.

I crafted this book to guide you, the parent, through the nuanced journey of raising an autistic child, starting from the crucial moment of post-diagnosis. Here, you won't find just a collection of strategies; you'll find a blend of evidence-based practices intertwined with personal stories from our community, all aimed at fostering understanding, resilience, and growth. My approach is holistic, balancing traditional medical advice with mindfulness, self-compassion, and creative expression to support not just your child's development but also your family's well-being.

This book seeks to acknowledge the spectrum of experiences unique to each family. It offers adaptable advice that grows with your child—from managing early behavioral challenges to navigating the complexities of social interactions and educational settings as they age toward puberty. Each chapter builds on the last, providing practical tools and insights into the strengths that autism can bring to your family's life.

As we move through these pages together, I hope you will encounter stories that mirror your own, offering solace and sparks of inspiration. These narratives are intended to help remind you that while the path may be difficult, you are not walking it alone. The strategies and insights shared here are flexible and designed to help you understand how to apply them to fit your child and family's unique needs and strengths.

I invite you to join me with an open heart and mind. Let's explore these pages together, learn from the community, and strengthen our resolve to meet the challenges and celebrate the victories ahead. This book is meant to be a companion on your journey, reaffirming the promise that despite the challenges, there is immense hope and numerous possibilities for joy and growth.

Together, let's embrace this path, equipped not just with strategies but also with a shared understanding and solidarity. Your journey is unique, and so, too, will your experience with this book. Let it be a source of hope, a tool for learning, and a testament to the incredible resilience and love that define the life of parenting an autistic child.

Chapter 1

Your Family and Autism - Understanding the Basics

From the first moment you hear the word 'autism' connected to your child, a flood of questions and emotions may surge through you. Some of those early days can feel like navigating a labyrinth without a map. However, with each step you take, you gather more knowledge, tools, and confidence, transforming you into a guide for your child, an advocate, and a learner in the expansive world of autism.

This chapter aims to lay the groundwork for your understanding of autism, dispelling myths and highlighting the nuances of the spectrum. We will build on and expand our knowledge of these foundational elements throughout the rest of the book.

Decoding Autism: Key Concepts and Misconceptions

When we discuss the autism spectrum, imagine a vast range of colors, each representing different abilities, challenges, and ways of experiencing the world. Autism is indeed a spectrum, with each individual presenting a unique combination of traits that can vary significantly from one person to another. This diversity means that two children, even within the same family, both diagnosed as autistic, can have very different strengths, needs, and challenges. For example, while one child might have significant challenges with verbal communication, another might speak fluently but struggle with social interactions, as with my girls.

Studies estimate that 90% of autistic individuals experience hypersensitivities to sounds, lights, or textures, which can be overwhelming and sometimes painful.

Understanding sensory sensitivities is also pivotal. Recognizing signs of sensory overload is key to creating supportive environments. For example, a child might cover their ears in a noisy cafeteria, or they might avoid specific clothing because of its texture. Awareness of these sensitivities allows you to make modifications, such as providing noise-canceling headphones or choosing soft, seamless clothing. Properly addressing your child's sensory sensitivities can not only improve your child's comfort but also have a positive impact on their behavior, communication, and social skills development.

One of the most vital concepts to understand for your child's well-being is masking. Masking refers to the process by which autistic individuals hide their autistic characteristics to blend into social settings. While this may sound beneficial for managing specific social situations, it often results in considerable mental fatigue and stress. This is why it is crucial to eliminate any request that your child alter their behavior to blend in.

SOCIAL EXPECTATIONS VS MASKING

There is a distinct difference between the general practice of adapting behavior based on the social environment—such as demonstrating politeness— and the intensive effort required by autistic people to seem neurotypical. This latter behavior demands continuous attention and self-regulation, draining mental energy and potentially increasing feelings of loneliness. Creating and finding environments where your autistic child feels safe to express themselves authentically, without the pressure to mask, is vital. These environments reduce the mental toll associated with masking and promote psychological well-being and a sense of belonging. Encouraging your child to be authentic while understanding basic social rules allows for genuine connections and supports mental health.

Dispelling myths about autism is equally important as understanding the spectrum itself. One common myth is that autistic individuals do not experience emotions. This is not true. Autistic individuals may experience and express their feelings differently, but this does not mean they do not feel them deeply. Another prevalent myth is that all autistic individuals possess extraordinary abilities in specific areas. While some individuals have remarkable talents, this is not a general rule for everyone diagnosed with autism. Believing in these myths can lead to unrealistic expectations and misconceptions, hindering the development of a supportive and understanding relationship with your autistic child and other autistic individuals.

Understanding these basics creates a strong foundation for your ongoing learning and adaptation as a parent. Each piece of knowledge brings you closer to providing the supportive, understanding environment your child needs to thrive.

The Family Journey Post-Diagnosis: Setting the Emotional Stage

When the diagnosis is first delivered, it's like standing at the edge of an unfamiliar ocean. The waves of emotions can hit hard—denial, fear, confusion, and sometimes relief that there's finally an explanation for the challenges you've been facing. It's okay to feel a whirlwind of emotions; it's natural and expected. Processing each feeling is a step towards understanding and acceptance.

As part of this whirlwind, many parents also experience a period of grief, mourning the future they envisioned for their child before diagnosis. This grief is legitimate and needs space to be acknowledged. It's essential to allow yourself to feel these emotions and to sit with them without judgment. Remember, accepting your child's diagnosis is not a concession to limitations; it's a pivotal step in embracing your family's unique journey. It's about recognizing the situation for what it is and seeking the most effective ways to support your child's growth and happiness.

Becoming and staying informed about autism plays a pivotal role in adapting to your family's evolving dynamics post-diagnosis. Embracing knowledge as a tool empowers you to navigate the emotions of daily challenges with a new perspective. A wealth of resources, including specialized books, informative websites, and dedicated organizations, are available to deepen your understanding of autism. Engaging with these resources enlightens you about your child's unique experience and guides you in providing the support they and the family need to flourish.

In navigating these initial emotions, building emotional resilience becomes crucial. Emotional resilience doesn't mean you won't have difficult days; it equips you to recover from these challenges more effectively. Techniques such as mindfulness, which involves being present in the moment and accepting things without judgment, can be incredibly helpful. Regularly engaging in activities that replenish your emotional energy, whether a hobby, exercise or connecting with friends, is also vital. Remember, taking care of yourself is not an act of selfishness; it's a necessity that enables you to be there for your child over the long haul.

As you adjust to this new reality, seeking support becomes more critical. This is a path to walk with others. Learning to advocate for your child's needs is a skill that will be developed over time. Whether negotiating with schools, finding suitable therapies, or ensuring your child's rights are respected, advocacy is an ongoing process. In Chapter 7, we will discuss strategies to connect with communities and professionals who can help lighten your load.

Considering your child's future can also stir deep emotions, especially when it leads to conversations about wills, trusts, and guardianship. The thought of delving into these legal matters might feel overwhelming at first. However, these steps are vital in ensuring your child's future security and well-being. By incorporating such measures into your family's planning, you safeguard your child's interests and find peace of mind in knowing their needs will continue to be met. We'll delve into these essential topics more broadly in Chapter 8, focusing on long-term planning. This isn't merely about financial security; it's about laying a foundation supporting your child's ability to flourish.

Navigating life post-diagnosis can be a path marked by emotional challenges but also immense growth and unexpected joys. As you learn to set the emotional stage for this new chapter of your family's life, remember that all your feelings are valid, support is available, and empowerment begins with education. By taking these steps, you are laying down the stones on which you and your family will tread, building a life filled with understanding, resilience, and love.

Sibling Relationships: Fostering Understanding and Support for Everyone

When we consider the dynamics within a family where one or more children have autism, it's crucial to recognize the experiences of their siblings. These children often navigate their own unique challenges and opportunities within the family unit. Parents need to cultivate an environment where all children feel valued and understood, ensuring that neurotypical siblings actively participate in the family's adaptive journey. Promoting inclusivity among siblings involves more than merely encouraging them to play together; it requires fostering a deep understanding and empathy for each other's experiences.

Involving siblings in caregiving in ways that resonate with their age and comprehension is a crucial strategy. This involvement might range from simple tasks, like helping with daily routines, to joining therapy sessions to learn supportive strategies. Equally important is engaging in open and age-appropriate conversations about autism, which not only educates but also demystifies autism-related behaviors, thereby easing any fears or misunderstandings. It's equally critical to cultivate each child's individual interests and independence within the family's structure. Encouraging each to follow their interests and activities allows them to grow on their own terms, underscoring their unique role in the family's collective journey.

Support groups for siblings can be invaluable. These groups provide a safe space where siblings can express their feelings, share experiences, and learn from others facing similar situations. If no such groups exist in your area, consider starting one. Chapter 7 delves deeper into starting a support group.

It's not uncommon for siblings of autistic children to experience feelings of jealousy and resentment. These emotions typically arise from observing the seemingly unequal division of parental attention or disruptions to family routines that cater to the needs of the autistic sibling. Openly addressing these feelings with empathy and understanding is essential.

Parents can encourage a family dialogue that allows each child to voice their emotions without fear of judgment. Embracing the concept of 'holding space' for each other's feelings is a significant step in acknowledging and validating these emotions. Additionally, allocating one-on-one time with each sibling ensures they feel seen and appreciated. Incorporating activities promoting mutual respect and understanding, such as collaborative projects or family games emphasizing teamwork and cooperation, can further strengthen the family bond.

Celebrating each child's achievements is pivotal in fostering a positive family environment. Each sibling's successes, whether in academia, sports, arts, or personal milestones, must be acknowledged and celebrated with equal enthusiasm. This practice helps to build a family culture where all achievements, big or small, are valued. It reinforces the idea that while the family may navigate the world of autism together, they also recognize and cheer for each individual's journey and accomplishments.

Through these approaches, parents can nurture a family dynamic that supports the growth and development of all children, fostering relationships built on understanding, respect, and mutual support. This not only enhances the quality of life for the sibling without autism but also enriches the life of the autistic child, who benefits immensely from the empathy and companionship of their sibling.

Crafting a Home Environment That Supports Neurodiversity

Creating a home that caters to the needs of an autistic child while still accommodating the rest of the family requires a thoughtful balance between structure and flexibility. The goal is to foster a space where your child feels safe and understood, a sanctuary that minimizes anxiety and supports their unique way of interacting with the world.

Imagine a home where every element, from the lighting to the layout, is thoughtfully curated to reduce sensory overload, which can be a frequent challenge for those on the spectrum. Soft lighting, minimal clutter, and quiet spaces can significantly decrease daily stress for a sensory-sensitive child. Consider the materials used in your furniture or the paint on your walls. Opt for textures and colors that are soothing and not overly stimulating. It's about creating an environment where your child can feel secure and at peace, promoting a sense of safety that extends to every corner of their living space.

Routine and structure are often vital for autistic individuals, providing a predictable and secure framework that can help mitigate the anxiety associated with the unknown. Structured routines, like regular mealtimes, bedtime rituals, and scheduled playtime, can help your autistic child understand what to expect each day, significantly easing their stress. However, life is unpredictable, and changes are inevitable. To help your child cope with unexpected changes, gradually introduce slight variations in their routine in a controlled manner. This could be as simple as taking a different route when walking to the park or rearranging a room's layout. The key is to make these changes gradually and predictably, ensuring your child feels supported throughout the process.

Explaining changes in advance and discussing them openly can help reduce any potential anxiety. These moments of flexibility are not just about teaching adaptability; they are also opportunities to explore and learn about new experiences together, reinforcing that change can be positive and not something to fear. We go deeper into this in Chapter 3.

Visual aids can be incredibly helpful in reinforcing the structure of the environment while promoting independence. Visual schedules, for example, use pictures to represent different parts of the day—from brushing teeth to school time to playtime. These visuals help make abstract concepts more concrete and understandable. Labels can also be a great tool, especially for children who are non-verbal or are still developing their reading skills. Labeling items around the house, from toy bins to food items, helps your child navigate their environment independently and confidently. These visual cues act as reminders and empower your child to participate more fully in daily activities. They provide a clear, visual pathway through their day-to-day tasks, reducing anxiety and boosting their self-esteem as they accomplish each task independently.

Creating a home that supports neurodiversity isn't just about adapting physical spaces—it's about building an atmosphere of acceptance and understanding. It's a continuous process of learning what works best for your child and family, making adjustments as needed, and celebrating the small successes. As you mold your living space to meet the needs of your autistic child, you also pave the way for a family life that is more harmonious, understanding, and deeply connected.

Balancing Parental Expectations with Reality

Setting realistic goals for your autistic child is more like steering a boat with a very sensitive rudder—minor adjustments can make significant changes in direction, and it's all about finding the right balance. When you start to set goals, it's vital to anchor them in the reality of your child's capabilities and their pace of development. It's not about lowering your expectations but aligning them in a way that encourages progress without setting the bar out of reach. For instance, if your child struggles with verbal communication, a realistic initial goal could be using simple gestures or sign language to express needs rather than forming complete sentences.

Celebrating these small victories is crucial. Each little success, be it a new word, a shared glance, or a peaceful mealtime, is a stepping stone towards more significant achievements, and acknowledging these moments fuels both your child's confidence and your resilience.

Adjusting parental expectations doesn't just benefit your child; it can significantly change how you experience your role as a parent. It's about evolving with your child's development. As they grow and master new skills, your expectations will naturally shift. This dynamic process keeps you both moving forward but requires you to stay observant and responsive to their progress. For example, if your child has mastered sorting objects by color, the next step could be sorting by size or shape, slowly building on existing skills to expand their abilities. This approach ensures that your expectations are always in sync with their current capabilities, providing a continuous challenge that is neither overwhelming nor under-stimulating.

Navigating societal pressures and judgments can be one of the more challenging aspects of parenting an autistic child. The playground, the grocery store, family gatherings—these everyday environments can become arenas of scrutiny. Unsolicited advice or critical remarks can come from well-meaning strangers, acquaintances, and even family, often based on a limited understanding of autism. Developing a strategy to handle these situations is essential.

One effective method is to prepare a few responses you are comfortable with, such as "Thank you for your concern, but we have found a method that works well for us," or "I appreciate your input, and every child is different. What works for one may not work for another." These responses assert your confidence in your parenting and politely disengage from potentially unproductive conversations. Remember, you know your child best, and a deep understanding of their needs informs your choices.

Embracing your child's individuality is perhaps the most joyful aspect of this journey. Every autistic child brings a unique perspective and set of talents to the world. Celebrating these attributes amidst a society that often values conformity can be a profound act of love and acceptance. It's about seeing your child not just for the challenges they face but for the complete person they are—quirks, talents, struggles, and all. This could mean encouraging their unusual interests, like collecting sticks from every park visit or lining up cars by color rather than racing them. These unique traits make your child who they are, and when embraced, they often reveal hidden depths and abilities. By valuing these distinctive aspects, you bolster their self-esteem and advocate for a broader acceptance of neurodiversity in your community.

Remember, balancing expectations with reality is not about curtailing hopes or dreams; it's about grounding them in a profound understanding of your child's unique developmental landscape. It's a balance that requires patience, observation, and, most importantly, celebrating small successes. As you adjust your expectations and learn to navigate external pressures, you also learn to appreciate and champion your child's individuality, crafting a path that respects their pace and personhood. This balance isn't static; it shifts and grows as you and your child do, always pointing towards new horizons and possibilities.

Learning from Our Challenges

When we open up about the ups and downs of raising autistic children, we find a shared language of resilience and hope that binds us, regardless of our backgrounds. In sharing these personal stories, we can uncover not just the challenges but the profound joys and unexpected victories of raising an autistic child. For example, I recall a friend recounting the first time her daughter used sign language to tell her, "I love you." She described the overwhelming moment of sheer joy resulting from countless hours of communication therapy - a true testament to the power of perseverance and love. Such stories are not just heartwarming; they are a reminder of what is possible for parents who might feel they are facing insurmountable challenges.

Stories like this remind us that life is about more than just coping; it's about thriving. It's finding joy in the small moments, like the spontaneous hugs or the giggles over a favorite book. It's seeing your child overcome a challenge, no matter how small, and knowing that each step forward is a victory. These stories do more than provide comfort—they forge a path of resilience, teaching us that while the road may be challenging, it is filled with incredible joy and triumph.

Chapter 2

Cultivating Connection - Shaping Communication to Fit Your Child's Needs

Imagine a day when your child looks up at you, eyes gleaming with understanding, and you sense that invisible bridge of communication solidifying. It's those moments we live for, isn't it? Communication forms the core of human connection, and for our autistic children, it can often seem like a field strewn with obstacles. Yet, with patience, observation, and tailored strategies, these barriers can be transformed into pathways of understanding and expression. This chapter is dedicated to navigating these pathways, understanding your child's unique way of communicating, and adapting your approach to meet them right where they are.

Understanding Your Child's Communication Style

Discovering how your child communicates is like uncovering a secret language—one that is unique and special to just them. Every autistic child has their way of interacting with the world, and as parents, it's our job to become fluent in their language. For some, words may flow freely, while others might rely more on gestures, facial expressions, or other forms of non-verbal communication. Observing your child in different settings can provide crucial clues about their preferred methods of communication. Notice when they are most communicative— perhaps during a particular activity they enjoy, like drawing or playing with trains. These observations can help you understand when they are most comfortable and when communication comes more easily.

Body language and tone often speak louder than words, especially for non-verbal children. Learning to interpret these signals can be like decoding a complex dance, where every movement and every look holds meaning. Does your child avoid eye contact when overwhelmed, or perhaps seek physical closeness when they need reassurance? These cues, subtle as they may be, are powerful communicators. Responding appropriately to them can enhance your connection and help your child feel understood and supported. For example, acknowledging and positively reinforcing natural expressions, such as hand gesturing when excited, can bolster your child's confidence in their unique way of communicating.

Professional assessments can be invaluable in mapping out your child's communication landscape. Speech-language pathologists and autism specialists can provide insights into your child's communication abilities and recommend strategies to enhance their skills. These assessments, which should be considered when you notice your child struggling with new or existing communication challenges, can serve as a guiding star, helping to align your strategies with your child's developmental needs. They can offer a professional perspective that complements your parental intuition, giving you a fuller picture of your child's communication abilities.

Tailoring your approach to communication is not about changing your child's way of interacting but rather adjusting your methods to better align with theirs. This might mean simplifying your language and using fewer words or increasing your use of gestures and visual aids. For example, if your child better understands instructions when they are demonstrated rather than explained, take the time to show them what you mean with clear, simple actions. This adjustment in your communication style can significantly affect how effectively you and your child can connect and understand each other.

As you navigate the complexities of communication with your child, remember that every step forward, no matter how small, is a leap toward more profound connection and understanding. By observing, adapting, and responding with empathy and patience, you create a communicative environment that respects and nurtures your child's unique way of expressing themselves. Each day, you'll find that your ability to speak and understand this unique language grows, bringing moments of joy and a profound sense of connection.

Navigating Non-Verbal Communication: Beyond Words

In the tapestry of communication, words are just one thread; gestures, expressions, and sensory cues hold together the rest, creating a rich, textured understanding between you and your child. The beautiful complexity of non-verbal communication opens up myriad pathways for connection, especially when traditional spoken language might not be your child's primary mode of expression. Let's look at these methods, enhancing how you connect and communicate and ensuring that each gesture and glance can weave a stronger bond between you and your child.

Gestures and Sign Language

Gestures, embodying the grace of hands and body, play a pivotal role in enriching communication. Teaching your child the language of gestures and becoming fluent in their non-verbal cues is akin to mastering a new dance. It begins with the basics—pointing to express interest, waving as a greeting or farewell, nodding to signal agreement, and shaking the head for disagreement. These foundational gestures pave the way for more intricate expressions that convey a spectrum of needs and emotions. By actively observing and reflecting your child's gestures, and encouraging the discovery of new ones, you foster a deeper level of non-verbal communication between you.

Integrating sign language weaves an additional, vibrant thread into the communication tapestry, serving as a powerful and reassuring form of expression when words are elusive. This visually rich language, with its array of signs and gestures, enables your child to convey complex thoughts and emotions in an accessible way. By embracing this mutual language, you deepen your bond and foster an understanding that transcends words, enriching your interactions with a dynamic interplay of movement and meaning that resonates with both of you.

Facial Expressions

Facial expressions are the silent storytellers of our inner world. Teaching your child to read and use facial expressions can open up new avenues for understanding emotions in communication—both their own and those of others.

DAILY APPLICATION

Start with the most basic emotions: happiness, sadness, anger, and surprise.

Use exaggerated expressions to depict an emotion and pair it with a situation that might typically evoke such a reaction. For instance, widen your eyes and mouth to express surprise when you find their favorite toy in an unexpected place.

Over time, using facial expressions for communication in daily life helps your child connect these expressions to real-life scenarios, enhancing their ability to read social cues and interact more meaningfully with others. This skill not only aids in social interactions but also helps build empathy, a crucial aspect of emotional development.

The Importance of Sensory Integration

The role of sensory integration in communication is often overlooked, yet it is crucial. Sensory sensitivities can significantly impact how your child perceives and interacts with their environment, which in turn affects their communication. For instance, a child overwhelmed by sensory inputs such as noise or light might struggle to focus on a conversation or maintain eye contact. Recognizing these sensitivities and creating a sensory-friendly environment can help reduce these barriers. Strategies such as providing a quiet space for conversations or using soft, calming colors in your communication aids can make a significant difference. Additionally, integrating sensory activities that align with your child's needs into your daily routine can improve their sensory integration, making communication less stressful and more effective.

DAILY APPLICATION

Meal Time Sensory Integration

Use mealtime to allow your child to explore their senses safely by incorporating sensory-friendly foods and eating practices into meals. (Adapt the example below to fit your child's sensitivity needs.)

An example for a child who is sensitive to textures.

Serve a mix of familiar and new foods in small, manageable portions. This allows your child to explore different textures at their own pace. One way I used to do this with my girls was to serve each food separately in sections of a muffin tin.

Understanding and adapting to the nuances of non-verbal communication enhances your ability to connect with your child and empowers them to express their thoughts and feelings more freely and fully. As you explore and implement these strategies, you'll likely discover that each small step in learning these non-verbal cues and tools is a leap towards richer, more fulfilling interactions.

The Role of Augmentative and Alternative Communication (AAC) in Everyday Life

For nonverbal autistic children, technology has emerged as a transformative force, turning unspoken thoughts into spoken words and shared emotions. In today's tech-driven world, gadgets and apps can become voices for those who would otherwise navigate life in silence. This is where Augmentative and Alternative Communication (AAC) devices come into play as crucial tools that bridge the communication gap. Speech-generating devices, for instance, range from simple button-based machines that utter preset phrases to sophisticated systems that allow users to construct sentences and engage in conversations. These devices are not just about facilitating basic needs; they enable your child to share thoughts, make choices, and even crack jokes. Communication apps on tablets and smartphones offer customizable interfaces and the ability to carry them anywhere, making communication fluid and more accessible outside the confines of the home.

Integrating AAC devices into everyday life can profoundly impact your family's interactions. Each type of AAC device serves a different purpose and suits different needs.

Picture Exchange Communication Systems (PECS®): Bridging the Communication Gap

At the heart of augmentative and alternative communication lies the Picture Exchange Communication System (PECS®), a method designed with simplicity and efficacy in mind. PECS® empowers nonverbal autistic children by enabling them to express their needs, desires, and feelings through the physical exchange of picture cards. These cards, which depict various items, activities, and emotions, serve as tangible tools for children to initiate communication without needing speech.

The process begins with the child handing a picture of a desired item to a communication partner, who immediately honors the request. This exchange reinforces the power of communication, providing a clear, tangible outcome for the child's effort. Over time, children learn to string together pictures to form simple sentences, further enhancing their ability to convey more complex thoughts and requests.

PECS® is more than just a communication tool; it's a stepping stone toward developing richer, more complex forms of expression. By starting with concrete, visual forms of communication, PECS® opens the door to further linguistic and social development. For many families, PECS® has been a breakthrough, transforming frustration and silence into interaction and engagement.

Speech Generating Devices

Speech-generating devices stand as powerful allies, offering a voice to those who might otherwise be without one. These devices range in complexity from simple, one-touch systems that articulate basic needs or desires to advanced technology capable of synthesizing speech in real-time, allowing for fluid, dynamic conversation. On the other hand, text-based applications are particularly beneficial for older children and teenagers who may be experts at typing yet find verbal communication challenging. These apps transform typed text into spoken words, bridging the gap between thought and speech. Beyond mere communication, these tools provide a platform for self-expression, enabling users to share their thoughts, stories, and humor with the world around them.

These tools are not just stopgaps until speech develops; in many cases, they enhance language skills by providing a platform for safe, stress-free communication. Importantly, studies have shown that AAC devices can encourage speech development rather than hinder it, as they reduce the pressure and frustration often associated with verbal communication, creating a more relaxed learning environment.

For AAC devices to be effective, however, family members must be adept at using them. This means training is essential —not just a one-time tutorial but ongoing education to keep up with updates and new features. Consistency across all environments—home, school, and social settings—is crucial to reinforce learning and usability. For instance, if a child uses a speech-generating device at home, ensuring that their school and therapy settings are equipped and knowledgeable about the same device supports continuity in communication development.

Real-Life Applications of AAC

Consider the story of Emma, a 6-year-old girl who, before introducing an AAC device, showed immense frustration during interactions. One day at school, Emma became so frustrated that she kicked a classroom trashcan and sent it flying across the room. After consulting with the school and Emma's therapy team, her family introduced a tablet with a speech-generating app tailored to her needs. This allowed her to express her needs, feelings, and thoughts. The immediate difference was not just in Emma's ability to communicate but also in her behavior—fewer tantrums and more smiles. Her teachers used the same setup at school, ensuring she could participate in class discussions. Social gatherings also became less daunting as Emma could now 'speak' her mind and engage with peers and relatives more meaningfully.

Customizable apps, like the one Emma used, are another layer of AAC that offers flexibility to meet individual needs. These apps allow parents and therapists to create and modify the content, such as adding new words, customizing the layout, and even integrating personal photos, making the device more personal and engaging for the child. For example, an app could be customized to include pictures of the child's favorite toys or family members, making the process of requesting enjoyable and familiar.

What AAC device is suitable for my child?

Many factors need to be considered when evaluating the effectiveness of a communication app or tool. One of the best places to look is verified user reviews. Feedback from professional therapists can also guide recommendations and adjustments, ensuring the choice remains a viable tool for your child.

Consider the following when evaluating an AAC device:

- What insights do the user reviews provide?
- Will every family member understand how to use it easily?
- Will it help reduce frustration?
- Can the app/device grow with your child's developing skills?
- Does it match your child's cognitive and communication needs?

Navigating AAC options can be daunting, but the benefits of finding the right fit are immeasurable. As you explore these technologies, you empower your child to own their voice, engage with the world on their terms, and, most importantly, express their personality and thoughts.

Practical Tips for Encouraging Verbal Communication

The sounds of early verbalization, whether babbles, giggles, or attempts at words, are like music to a parent's ears. Every sound your child makes is a stepping stone toward language development, and there are delightful ways to nurture these vocalizations further.

Creating opportunities for verbal interaction throughout the day is crucial in encouraging verbal communication. These ongoing verbal engagements expose your child to language in its natural context, making language learning a constant, immersive experience.

Create a Language-Rich Environment

Building a language-rich environment is about more than just words; it's about creating a space that invites curiosity and communication. Here are some examples of language-rich activities you can build into your interactions with your child:

Reading: One of the most joyful and effective ways to do this is through reading together. Choose books with large, colorful pictures and simple text that draw attention and stimulate interest. As you read, point to pictures and describe them, ask questions, and encourage any attempt your child makes to articulate words or sounds.

Singing: Singing is another magical tool in your communication toolkit. Songs with repetitive and simple melodies are enchanting to children. They often contain rhymes, and a clear rhythm can make language easier to grasp. Plus, the repeated phrases in songs provide a fun way for children to practice language without the pressure of formulating sentences on their own.

Descriptive Talk: As you go about your day, engaging in descriptive talk transforms everyday moments into learning opportunities. Describe your actions, the environment, and your emotions. This builds vocabulary and helps your child connect words to the world around them.

Using Speech Therapy at Home

Speech therapy techniques can often be seamlessly integrated into daily routines, empowering you to consistently support your child's communication development at home. These practices gradually help build confidence and skills, fostering a positive learning environment.

One basic technique is the use of clear, direct language. When speaking with your child, use short sentences and highlight the essential words. This clear way of speaking aids your child in understanding and processing information, serving as a template for the type of speech they may begin to imitate. Another technique is the strategic use of pauses. After asking a question or saying something to your child, give them plenty of time to respond. These pauses are crucial; they signal to your child that it's their turn to speak and provide the necessary space for them to respond. For children just starting to talk, consider focusing on sounds and syllables rather than whole words. Break down words into more manageable parts and celebrate any attempt at repetition.

DAILY APPLICATION

Sound Mimicry Play

Mimicking sounds might seem simple, but it's profoundly effective. As part of your daily play time, use sound repetition to help make verbalization fun.

When your child makes a sound, enthusiastically repeat it to them. If they make the sound again, repeat it.

When your child changes the sound, you change with them.

This not only shows that you are listening and engaged, but it also encourages them to continue experimenting with sounds. Over time, this playful echoing can become a form of conversation, helping your child understand the rhythm and turn-taking involved in communication.

Patience and positive reinforcement are the golden threads that run through all these strategies. The path to verbal communication can be slow and filled with challenges, and it's natural to feel impatient or discouraged sometimes. However, it's important to celebrate every effort your child makes to communicate, no matter how small or unclear. Each attempt is a significant achievement and a stepping stone towards more complex communication. Positive reinforcement can be as simple as a smile, a clap, or a cheerful comment like "I heard you!" or "Well done!" These affirmations make the learning process enjoyable and motivating for your child, and they reinforce the value of their efforts. Remember, the goal is to build confidence and skills over time, not to rush the process. Your support, encouragement, and acknowledgment of your child's efforts are crucial to their success in developing verbal communication skills.

Success Stories of Communication Breakthroughs

In autism, each family's story adds a rich layer to our understanding of communication. These stories are not just narratives; they are testaments to resilience, innovation, and the profound impact of tailored communication strategies. Across diverse backgrounds, families discover unique pathways to connect with their children, highlighting the universal quest for understanding and the joy of breakthrough moments.

Take the case of Sofia, a young girl who lives in a bilingual home. Initially, Sofia used very few words and communicated mainly by pulling her parents towards objects of interest. Her speech therapist suggested incorporating both languages in therapy sessions. As music held deep cultural significance for the family, they also incorporated music. Songs in both languages were used to help Sofia associate words with actions and emotions.

This dual-language approach not only respected the family's cultural identity but also engaged Sofia in a joyful and familiar medium. Over time, Sofia began to use words from both languages to express her needs and even sing short phrases from her favorite songs. This breakthrough was significant, not just in terms of language development but in fostering a deeper connection with her heritage and her family.

Another inspiring story is that of Zachary, who faced significant challenges in social interactions due to his difficulty reading facial expressions and body language. His team of teachers implemented a game-based intervention, where Zachary used an app designed to help children recognize and mimic expressions. The app used a camera to capture and reflect his facial movements, providing immediate feedback and rewards for correct imitations. This interactive method turned a challenging area of communication into a fun activity.

Over several months, Zachary's ability to interpret expressions improved remarkably, which had a ripple effect on his social interactions. His teachers reported an increase in positive social engagements, and Zachary seemed more confident during group activities. The change in his social life was profound, illustrating how addressing one aspect of communication can enhance a child's overall quality of life.

These stories underscore the importance of personalized communication strategies that consider your child's environment, interests, and individual challenges. The impact of these tailored approaches extends beyond mere conversation; they foster self-expression, confidence, and happier, more connected lives. Experts in the field emphasize the necessity of continuous adaptation and customization of communication strategies. They advocate for an ongoing assessment and tweaking of methods to align with your child's evolving needs and capabilities, ensuring that your child can reach their full communication potential.

These community stories highlight the successes and the collaborative effort required among parents, therapists, and educators. They remind us that communication is a dynamic skill, with its development being a continuous journey of adjustments, learning, and, most importantly, understanding.

As we close this chapter on communication breakthroughs, we are reminded of the transformative power of effective communication strategies. Each story shared here threads into the larger narrative of hope and potential that defines the journey of raising autistic children. With each breakthrough, whether small or significant, we see the undeniable impact of patience, creativity, and personalized approaches in unlocking the world of communication for autistic children.

Now, we transition from the exploration of enhancing communication skills to the realm of compassionate behavior support strategies. This next chapter is designed to guide you through the delicate process of understanding and managing behaviors in a way that respects the individuality and needs of your autistic child. Here, we will delve into evidence-based approaches and practical strategies emphasizing empathy, respect, and patience to foster a supportive environment that encourages positive behaviors and emotional growth.

Chapter 3
Behavioral Support - Thoughtful Approaches to Managing Meltdowns and Beyond

Imagine a day that begins with laughter and exploration but suddenly shifts as your child encounters something unsettling, something that you might not even notice. A tag on the back of a shirt, a sudden loud noise, or a break from routine – small triggers that can lead to significant distress. As parents, understanding these triggers and learning how to manage and prevent meltdowns is like assembling a puzzle; each piece provides more clarity and control, leading to a more peaceful and enjoyable life for your child and your entire family.

Is It a Tantrum or a Meltdown?

Distinguishing between a tantrum and a meltdown is crucial in tailoring your approach to support your child effectively. Tantrums are often a child's strategic response to not getting what they want and are usually aimed at an audience. They have a certain level of control over a tantrum and may stop once their goal is achieved or they realize it won't be met. In contrast, meltdowns are not within the child's control and are not used to manipulate a situation. They are a response to overwhelming stress or sensory overload and continue regardless of whether anyone is present. Understanding this distinction is the first step in managing and preventing these intense situations.

Identifying Triggers and Preventing Meltdowns

Recognizing the early signs of an impending meltdown involves keen observation and understanding of your child's unique cues. These signs can be subtle—a slight furrow of the brow, clenching of fists, or even a particular stare. By tuning into these early signals, you can intervene before emotions escalate to a meltdown. It's about developing a sixth sense, attuned to your child's non-verbal language, which speaks volumes about their internal state. This keen observation allows you to address discomfort in its early stage, employing calming strategies that can help you navigate away from a potential meltdown.

Environmental triggers are often the culprits behind sudden behavioral changes. Common triggers include overwhelming sensory environments like loud, crowded places, unexpected changes in routine, or even discomfort caused by physical factors like bright lights, itchy fabrics, or sudden temperature changes. By identifying these triggers, you can create a tailored plan to mitigate them. For instance, if crowded spaces are a trigger, visiting places during off-peak hours or finding less crowded alternatives can make outings more enjoyable. If routine changes are unsettling, visual schedules or timers can help prepare your child for what's next, making transitions smoother and less anxiety-inducing.

Emotional regulation is a critical skill for all children, but especially for those on the autism spectrum who might find the world overwhelming. Techniques such as deep breathing exercises, sensory breaks with quiet time, or using sensory toys designed to calm, like weighted blankets or fidget toys, can be beneficial. These strategies help to regulate the nervous and sensory systems, providing a direct method for relaxing the body and mind. Integrating these techniques into your child's daily routine can empower them to manage their emotions proactively.

DAILY APPLICATION

Create a Self-Soothing Kit

Put together a small bag with your child's preferred sensory tools, such as stress balls, noise-canceling headphones, fidgets, or stuffies. Ensure your child has access to the bag in all environments so they can turn to it when they feel anxious or upset.

This can help your child feel more secure and empowered no matter where they are.

Proactive planning plays a pivotal role in preventing meltdowns and managing behavioral challenges. This involves not only preparing your child for upcoming changes but also preparing yourself and the environments you'll be navigating.

For instance, finding safe places your child can go when they feel overwhelmed can create a haven for calming their emotions. Additionally, researching in advance to see if venues offer "sensory guides" or quiet hours can make all the difference when planning outings. These guides provide insights into sensory-friendly times or areas, which can help in planning visits during less stimulating conditions.

Explaining the day's schedule to your child beforehand, using simple and straightforward language, can also help set expectations and reduce anxiety. For situations where sensory guides are unavailable, having a clear, visual itinerary of the day's activities can provide your child a sense of security and control, making unknown environments more navigable and less intimidating.

Navigating the world with an autistic child means being armed with strategies, insights, and a deep understanding of what can trigger discomfort for your child. Recognizing early signs of distress, managing environmental triggers, and using techniques to regulate emotions can prevent many meltdowns before they start. This proactive approach eases day-to-day challenges and empowers your child with tools to manage their emotions, fostering a sense of independence and confidence that will benefit them throughout their life. As you continue to adapt and refine these strategies, remember that each step forward is a step towards a more supportive environment for your child to thrive in.

Handling Public Meltdowns with Grace and Confidence

When you're out in the world with your child, the unpredictability of public spaces can sometimes lead to challenging situations. Handling a meltdown gracefully under the watchful eyes of the public can feel unnerving. You might worry about judgment from bystanders or feel stressed about quickly calming your child. However, with some thoughtful preparation and a few strategic techniques up your sleeve, you can confidently manage these incidents and help your child navigate them with as little distress and as much dignity as possible.

De-escalation techniques are crucial when a meltdown occurs. One effective strategy is distraction. If you sense your child becoming overwhelmed, gently try to redirect their attention to something they find enjoyable or calming. This could be a favorite game on your phone, pointing out something interesting in the environment, or engaging them in a beloved topic of conversation. If the situation escalates, don't hesitate to find a quiet spot where your child can calm down, away from crowds and noise. Sometimes, stepping away from the sensory overload can significantly reduce stress levels for both of you and give you and your child the space to employ your preferred emotional regulation techniques. Additionally, make sure to have your child's "self-soothing kit" with items such as noise-canceling headphones or a soothing tactile toy, which can help your child regain control over their emotions.

Educating the public about autism can also play a role in these moments. While it's not your responsibility to educate everyone you encounter, finding simple ways to increase understanding can sometimes make public outings more manageable. If someone appears curious or concerned, a brief explanation can go a long way. You might say something like, "My child is autistic, and sometimes loud noises can be too much for them." Most people respond positively to straightforward explanations and are more empathetic once they understand the situation. This helps in the moment and fosters greater awareness and kindness towards the autism community in general.

Finally, focusing on self-care is crucial after handling a public meltdown. These episodes can be emotionally draining, and it's important to acknowledge and address your feelings. Allow yourself time to decompress and engage in activities that restore your calm. This might mean taking a few minutes to breathe deeply, debriefing the incident with a supportive friend or partner, or engaging in a relaxing activity once you're home. Remember, maintaining your emotional well-being is essential for providing the best support for your child. Self-compassion is vital—remind yourself you're doing your best in a challenging situation. Reducing personal guilt and shame is not just beneficial for you but also models healthy emotional coping strategies for your child.

Handling meltdowns with grace and confidence doesn't mean they won't happen or that they'll always go smoothly. It means you're equipped with strategies to manage them effectively, understand the importance of preparation, and recognize the need for compassion toward your child and yourself. Each experience, challenge, and small victory enriches your collective ability to navigate the world together, fostering resilience and understanding in every step.

The Impact of Routine and Structure on Behavior

Step into the shoes of your child for a moment; the world is a whirlwind of stimuli, each moment brimming with sounds, sights, and changes that might seem trivial to neurotypical individuals but can be overwhelming for someone on the autism spectrum. This is where the magic of routine comes into play. Think of routine as a gentle, reassuring hand on your child's back, offering predictability in an unpredictable world. The security that routine provides can significantly diminish anxiety and enhance behavior, making daily life not just manageable but also enjoyable for your child.

Creating effective routines is not just about setting a schedule; it's about weaving a tapestry of consistency that aligns with your child's needs and your family's lifestyle. Begin by observing the times of day when your child is most alert, relaxed, or tired. Use these cues to structure activities that flow naturally with their internal rhythm. For instance, if your child is most energetic in the morning, schedule physically demanding activities like therapy sessions or outdoor play during these hours. Conversely, quieter activities like reading or drawing can be reserved for times when they are winding down. It's also crucial to incorporate consistent meal and sleep times into the routine, as regular eating and sleeping patterns can significantly impact behavior and mood.

However, life is inherently fluid, and flexibility within routines is essential for helping your child adapt to changes without undue stress. Start by introducing small changes in a controlled and predictable manner, as discussed in Chapter 1. For example, if you usually have lunch at noon but plan to attend a family gathering where lunch will be served later, prepare your child in advance by discussing the change. You can adjust any visual schedule you've established to reflect this shift and plan a small snack at the usual lunchtime to ease the transition. Over time, these small adjustments can help your child become more adaptable, reducing their anxiety about changes and increasing their ability to cope with new situations.

By understanding the profound impact of routine and structure and learning to implement and adjust these tools effectively, you pave the way for smoother days and less stressful experiences for your child and your family. The predictability of a well-crafted routine offers a framework within which your child can find comfort and security, while planned flexibility teaches them to navigate life's inevitable changes. This balanced approach fosters an environment where your child can thrive, developing the skills they need to face the world confidently.

Positive Reinforcement: A Guide to Effective Use

Diving into the world of positive reinforcement can feel like discovering a secret garden of growth and positivity for your child. At its core, positive reinforcement is about encouraging desired behaviors through rewarding outcomes, making it a powerful tool in guiding the behavior of autistic children. Understanding why this approach is effective can open new doors for you and your child, fostering an environment where positive behaviors flourish.

Positive reinforcement works by rewarding a child's behavior immediately after it occurs, making it more likely to happen again. This happens because the reward creates a pleasant association with the behavior for your child, embedding a sense that 'when I do this, something good happens.' It's a simple yet profound principle that taps into the basic human inclination toward seeking pleasure and avoiding pain. For children on the spectrum who may struggle with complex social cues or abstract consequences, positive reinforcement provides clear, tangible feedback on their actions, making it easier to understand and internalize the behaviors you want to encourage.

The types of positive reinforcers can vary widely depending on what motivates your child individually. For some, verbal praise like "Great job putting your toys away!" can light up their day, while for others, a sticker chart or the opportunity to engage in a preferred activity, such as extra time with a favorite book or toy, might be more effective. The key is identifying what truly resonates with your child - what makes them smile, engage, or show excitement? Observing their reactions to different rewards can guide you in choosing the most effective reinforcers. For instance, if your child loves music, perhaps playing their favorite song after they've successfully completed a task could serve as a powerful motivator. On the other hand, if your child is a tactile seeker, maybe a small sensory toy could be used as a reward for good behavior during outings.

Consistency in the application of positive reinforcement is crucial for its success. It helps establish a reliable link between the behavior you want to encourage and the reward, making your child's learning process clearer and faster.

Consistency means regularly rewarding desired behavior and ensuring that the rewards are only given explicitly for those behaviors. This consistency helps to clarify behavioral expectations and reinforces the learning cycle, making it easier for your child to understand and meet those expectations. For example, if the goal is for your child to learn to communicate their needs verbally, consistently rewarding each attempt – even if not perfectly executed – with praise or a tangible reward can reinforce their effort and encourage further attempts.

However, it's essential to distinguish positive reinforcement from negative reinforcement, as they can often be confused. Negative reinforcement involves the removal of an unpleasant stimulus to increase a behavior. For instance, turning off a loud disliked noise when a child eats their veggies might encourage them to eat, but it teaches them to behave in a certain way to avoid something negative rather than to achieve something positive. This method may result in behaviors that are only exhibited under certain uncomfortable conditions and typically does not cultivate true internal motivation to maintain a behavior. Positive reinforcement, by focusing on rewarding desirable behavior, promotes a more joyful and internally motivated path to learning and development.

By integrating positive reinforcement into your daily interactions with your child, you create a supportive atmosphere that enhances behavioral development and strengthens your bond. It's a strategy that celebrates big and small achievements and emphasizes the joys of learning and growing together. By consistently using carefully chosen reinforcers, you can help your child navigate the complexities of their world with confidence and success, backed by the knowledge that they are supported and cherished for every effort they make.

Customizing Behavior Support Plans

Navigating the nuances of behavior support for your autistic child can feel a bit like being a detective and a strategist all rolled into one. You're constantly piecing together clues about what best supports your child's needs. Customizing a behavior support plan isn't just helpful; it's crucial for fostering an environment where your child can thrive. The first step in this process is conducting a thorough assessment of your child's behavioral needs. This isn't something you have to do alone; involving your child's educators, therapists, and other caregivers ensures you have a well-rounded view of their behaviors across different settings. Each person involved might see different aspects of your child's behavior, providing insights that could be vital in crafting an effective support plan. Integrating these findings with your child's Individualized Education Program (IEP) can offer more structured support, aligning home strategies with educational goals. For more on integrating findings with an IEP, refer to Chapter 5.

The next critical step is setting specific, measurable, achievable, relevant, and time-bound (SMART) goals. These goals help transform your broad aspirations for your child's development into actionable steps. For example, if your child struggles with transitions between activities, a SMART goal could be, "By the end of the month, my child will move from playtime to mealtime with only one verbal reminder, demonstrated by doing so in four out of five instances." This goal is specific (focusing on transitions), measurable (one reminder, four out of five times), achievable (reasonable with practice), relevant (improves daily function), and time-bound (by the end of the month). Setting goals like this provides clear benchmarks for progress and success, which can be incredibly motivating for both you and your child.

Flexibility in your behavior plan is vital as your child grows and their needs evolve. What works one month might not work the next as they develop new skills or face different challenges. Regularly revisiting and revising the behavior plan ensures it remains aligned with their current needs. This might mean introducing new strategies or phasing out supports that are no longer necessary. For instance, as your child's verbal communication increases, you might shift focus from using visual language towards more complex verbal skills. This flexibility ensures the plan remains effective and helps your child progress without being held back by outdated strategies.

Documentation and tracking are the linchpins in understanding what's working and what isn't. Keeping detailed records of behaviors, the circumstances under which they occur, the strategies used, and the outcomes can provide a wealth of information over time. This documentation can be as simple as a daily log or as detailed as a behavior chart with notes on environmental factors. For busy working parents, leveraging technology can simplify this process. Consider using apps that allow you to quickly enter information on the go or set reminders to update your records at the same time each day to maintain consistency. These records become invaluable during assessments and reviews, providing clear evidence of what strategies have been effective and how your child's behavior has changed over time.

By carefully assessing needs, setting clear goals, maintaining flexibility, and diligently tracking the program, you create a dynamic and effective behavior support plan that grows with your child. This customized approach addresses the immediate behavioral needs and supports long-term development, ensuring that each step your child takes is supported by strategies that cater to their evolving needs. Remember, the goal of behavior support is not just about reducing undesirable behaviors—it's about empowering your child to reach their full potential, one step at a time.

Parental Testimonies

In the vast and varied experiences of families navigating autism, each story carries its own set of challenges, triumphs, and insights. These real-life stories not only shed light on practical behavior support but also showcase the diverse cultural backgrounds that shape different parenting styles. For instance, Maria, a mother from a large Italian family, shares how her cultural heritage's emphasis on strong family connections has helped her son's behaviors to grow and develop. By involving relatives in her son's care, she's been able to provide him with a consistent, loving environment that reinforces positive behaviors across different settings. She emphasizes her gratitude that family members have been willing to learn and grow their understanding of autism. This consistent sense of family support is a cornerstone of her approach.

On the other hand, John, who comes from a more reserved British background, stresses how structured routines and clear, consistent expectations are pivotal in his son's behavior support. He finds that a structured approach has helped his son navigate his days better and alleviated his parenting anxieties. Through trial and error, he's found that maintaining calm and consistency at home creates the safe space his son needs to understand and meet behavioral expectations. His story highlights how aligning behavior support strategies with personal and cultural parenting styles can support your child.

Parents have also shared various tips and tricks that have become invaluable in their behavior support toolkits. For example, Layla, a single mother, uses a reward system that includes a mix of verbal praise and tangible rewards. She's customized this system to include rewards specifically motivating for her daughter, such as extra reading time at night, which is her favorite activity. Verbal praise and tangible rewards are alternated because that approach works the best for her daughter. It took time and patience for Layla to find the unique combination that worked for both of them. Layla's approach underscores the importance of personalizing behavior support strategies to fit your child's unique interests and motivations, ensuring they are engaging and effective.

One of the most profound impacts of effective behavior support is its influence on family dynamics. Many parents have observed significant improvements not just in their child's life but in the overall family environment. Vikram shares how establishing a consistent routine has reduced daily conflicts and brought a sense of harmony to their home. By clearly communicating expectations and schedules, his family has experienced fewer misunderstandings and more cooperative interactions, enhancing the quality of their family life. This improvement in family dynamics often extends beyond the immediate family, positively affecting relationships with friends, extended family, and the community.

These testimonies from multiple families provide a panoramic view of the challenges and successes in behavior support within the autism community. They highlight the adaptability of strategies across different cultural contexts and underline the importance of customization in meeting individual needs. Most importantly, they show that while the path can be complex, the rewards of tailored behavior support strategies are profound, leading to enhanced family relationships and a better quality of life for all involved.

As we wrap up this chapter, we carry with us the real-life wisdom of these families navigating the daily realities of autism. Their experiences remind us that at the heart of behavior support is the pursuit of a harmonious, fulfilling family life. With each story, we see reflections of resilience, innovation, and the deep bonds that sustain families through their challenges. These narratives are more than just accounts of strategies and outcomes; they affirm the strength and love that parents bring to their roles each day.

In the next chapter, the focus shifts to social skill development. We'll explore the nuanced world of social interactions, the art of building friendships, and dealing with bullies, which can be challenging for autistic children. I aim to unravel these complexities, providing you with strategies that enhance your child's social comprehension and communication abilities.

Chapter 4

Fostering Social Skills - Making Friends and Dealing with Bullies

Navigating the social landscape can be a delightful yet complex journey for any child, and for those on the autism spectrum, the path can sometimes seem filled with more twists and turns. Picture this: a playground where groups of children are laughing, playing, and interacting. Somewhere in this lively scene is your child, possibly standing on the sidelines, perhaps unsure how to join in or communicate their desire to play. This chapter is designed to be your map through this intricate terrain, helping you guide your child in learning the dance of social interaction—a dance where every step, every gesture, and every look counts.

Assessing Social Skills: Starting Points

Embarking on the journey of enhancing your child's social skills begins with understanding where they currently stand. It's much like setting out on a hike: Knowing your starting point helps you plan the route and prepare for the challenges ahead. Social skills assessments, often provided by therapists, can offer a detailed evaluation of your child's social abilities. These assessments might include structured interactions and observations that help pinpoint strengths and areas for improvement. For example, they might assess how your child initiates communication with others, responds to social cues, or handles sharing and cooperation.

The insights from parents and teachers are equally crucial in this assessment. You and your child's teachers see different facets of their social interactions in different settings, from the classroom to the home and playground. Each environment brings out different aspects of your child's social repertoire. Using the Individualized Education Program (IEP) as a guide can be particularly insightful. The IEP often contains valuable observations from educational professionals about your child's social interactions and progress in school settings. It's a document that evolves, reflecting a growing understanding of your child's needs and abilities.

Setting realistic goals for social skills development is a delicate balance—it's about aiming for attainable progress that encourages your child to stretch beyond their current capabilities and avoids setting them up for frustration. For instance, if your child struggles with initiating conversation, a starting goal might be for them to respond to social approaches made by others rather than initiating interactions themselves. As they become comfortable with this, the next step could be encouraging them to ask a peer a simple question. These goals should build on each other, gradually stretching their abilities without overwhelming them.

Benchmarking progress in social skills is essential for maintaining direction and motivation. It's like marking the trail on a hike with waypoints. These benchmarks help you and your child see their progress, which is incredibly rewarding. They also allow you to adjust your strategies as needed, ensuring your child continues progressing. Establishing these benchmarks involves setting clear criteria for success and regularly reviewing your child's progress against them. This might mean noting improvements in how often your child appropriately takes turns in a conversation or the number of times they engage with peers during a week. Each small success is a step forward, a sign that your strategies are working and your child is developing the skills they need to navigate their social world more effectively.

Guiding the development of social skills is a significant part of raising an autistic child. It involves patience, persistence, and a lot of heart. Each child's path is unique, filled with its own challenges and triumphs. As you guide your child through the complex world of social interactions, remember that every effort you make builds towards a future where they can connect more deeply with the world around them. Now that we have a starting point let's explore strategies and tools to support you and your child on this journey, enhancing their ability to forge friendships and interact confidently with peers.

Role-Playing and Social Stories as Teaching Tools

Role-playing and social stories are like the rehearsal before the big play, providing your child with a safe space to practice and understand various social scenarios before encountering them in the real world.

Social Stories

Consider social stories as simple, clear narratives that illustrate specific social situations, breaking them into understandable and manageable parts. These stories help children grasp the nuances of social interactions, such as sharing toys or asking for help, by presenting them in a structured, predictable format. The key is to focus on the positive behaviors you want to encourage rather than those you wish to avoid.

Creating a Social Story

Choose a scenario your child often encounters or finds challenging.

Write the story using simple language and from your child's perspective.

Incorporate visuals to make the story more engaging and easier to understand.

An example of a social story for a child who struggles with greeting others might be:

> When I see someone I know, it is polite to say hello. I can smile, wave, or say 'hi' when I greet them. If I feel nervous, I can take a deep breath before speaking. Saying hello shows that I am friendly, and it helps others feel happy.

Role-Playing

Role-playing, on the other hand, allows your child to participate actively in a simulated interaction, giving them the opportunity to practice responses and actions in a controlled setting. This method is particularly beneficial because it enables your child to experiment with different ways of handling a situation, which can boost their confidence and improve their decision-making skills.

Implementing Role-Play

- Start by setting a specific scenario you want to work on, such as taking turns during a game.
- You can act out the roles with your child, switching roles occasionally to give them a chance to experience different perspectives.
- Use prompts and cues initially to guide your child, and gradually reduce these aids as they become more proficient.
- Celebrate their successful responses and gently guide them through the more challenging aspects, ensuring the experience remains positive and educational.

Example of a short role-play script designed to help a child riding the school bus practice what will happen when they get to school:

> **Bus Driver:** "Alright, we're at your school! Are
> you ready to get off?"
> **Child:** "Yes, I'm ready."
> **Bus Driver:** "Okay, make sure to hold the
> handrail and watch your step as you get off."
> **Child:** "Thank you!"
> **Bus Driver:** "You're welcome! Have a great day
> at school!"
> **Child:** "Thanks! I will!"

Integrating role-playing and social stories into your child's daily routine is crucial for reinforcing the skills they are learning. Try to incorporate these tools during regular play or set aside a specific daily time for social skills practice. Consistency is critical, as regular practice helps solidify the behaviors and skills being taught. Additionally, involving siblings or other family members in these activities can enhance the realism of the scenarios and encourage broader social interaction. This inclusion makes the activities more enjoyable and helps generalize the skills to various settings and people.

Customizing scenarios in role-playing and social stories is essential for maintaining their effectiveness and relevance. Tailor the scenarios to reflect situations your child will likely encounter in their everyday life and enhance the exercises' practical value. If your child has a school event coming up, for example, you could create a social story or role-play scenario about what might happen at the event, what kinds of interactions they might have, and how they can handle them. This preparation can help alleviate your child's anxiety about the event and equip them with the confidence to navigate it successfully.

Regularly employing role-playing and social stories will empower your child with the tools they need to understand and navigate the social world more effectively. These strategies provide a foundation for building robust social skills that can significantly enhance your child's ability to interact with others, making their daily experiences more enjoyable and fulfilling. As you continue to explore and utilize these tools, you'll likely discover just how transformative they can be in your child's social development.

Organizing Play Dates and Social Groups

When you're thinking about enriching your child's social experiences through play dates or social groups, the first step is selecting appropriate playmates. This is akin to choosing teammates in a cooperative game, where each player's strengths and styles contribute to the group's success. It's essential to find peers who understand your child's unique way of interacting and complement and enhance their social experiences. Look for children who exhibit patience, show a keen interest in other kids, or share similar interests with your child. These traits can make social interactions more enjoyable and less stressful for your child. Additionally, consider involving your child in groups like "Best Buddies," an organization that promotes friendships among children of all abilities, fostering an inclusive environment that is both supportive and enriching. The beauty of such organizations lies in their focus on mutual respect and understanding, which can significantly boost your child's confidence and social skills.

Structured play activities are another cornerstone of successful social interactions. These activities guide children through a shared goal while providing enough framework to reduce uncertainties that might arise during open-ended play. Think about activities that require cooperation, such as building a puzzle together, playing a board game that requires taking turns, or a simple art project that can be done in pairs. These structured activities not only keep the play focused and goal-oriented but also teach valuable social skills such as sharing, waiting for one's turn, and collaborative problem-solving. The predictability and clear rules associated with structured play can help reduce anxiety and make social interactions more manageable and enjoyable for autistic children.

Creating a supportive environment is crucial in ensuring these play dates go smoothly. This means setting up a physical space that minimizes distractions and sensory overload, which can be overwhelming for children on the spectrum. Choose a quiet, well-organized space for play dates, away from noisy household appliances or high-traffic areas. Soft lighting, minimal clutter, and calm colors can also help create a soothing environment. If your child is sensitive to noise, consider having a designated quiet area where they can go to regroup if they feel overwhelmed. This thoughtful setup makes the play space welcoming and significantly enhances your child's ability to focus and engage with others.

The role of adult supervision and facilitation cannot be overstated in making these social interactions positive and productive. While allowing children some autonomy to explore and interact at their own pace is important, gentle guidance from an adult can help navigate misunderstandings and steer interactions back on track when necessary. This might involve prompting children with phrases to use when they need to express their needs or feelings or stepping in to suggest alternative ways to resolve a conflict. The goal is not to control the play but to facilitate it so that all children feel included and able to participate fully. This supportive presence helps ensure that play dates are fun and rich opportunities for social learning and development.

Organizing play dates and social groups for your child involves thoughtful planning and active facilitation to ensure these experiences are positive and enriching. By carefully selecting playmates, structuring activities, creating a supportive environment, and providing appropriate adult supervision, you set the stage for your child to build meaningful friendships and develop crucial social skills. These gatherings are more than just play sessions; they are building blocks for your child's social development, crafted with intention and care.

Techniques for Building Empathy and Emotional Recognition

Empathy and emotional recognition are like the glue that holds human interactions together, allowing us to connect and understand each other on a deeper level. For autistic children, these skills can sometimes be challenging to develop, but with the right tools and guidance, you can help your child learn to navigate the emotional landscapes of themselves and others. Emotion cards or digital apps designed for emotional education can be excellent tools in this journey. These resources usually feature faces displaying different emotions or scenarios that prompt a child to identify what someone might be feeling. By regularly using these tools in a playful and engaging manner, your child can begin to recognize and label emotions effectively, which is the first step in understanding them.

Modeling expressive communication plays a pivotal role in teaching your child about emotions. Children learn a great deal from watching the adults around them. When you openly express your emotions, using words and corresponding non-verbal cues like facial expressions and body language, you provide clear models for your child to emulate. For instance, if you're feeling happy, articulate this emotion by saying, "I'm feeling happy because we're spending this time together," and accompany your words with a smile and open body language. This demonstration helps your child understand how emotions are expressed and encourages them to express their feelings openly and appropriately.

Incorporating games and activities that build empathy can also be a fun and effective way to enhance your child's emotional understanding. Emotion mirror games, where you make a face expressing an emotion and have your child mimic it, not only help in recognizing emotions but also in physically expressing them. Situation reaction role-plays, where you and your child act out different scenarios and discuss how each character might feel, can further deepen their understanding of emotional perspectives and consequences. For example, you could role-play a situation where one character receives a gift and another doesn't. Discuss how each character feels and what could be done to make everyone feel better. These activities encourage your child to put themselves in someone else's shoes, fostering empathy and consideration for others' feelings.

Daily Application

Using storytime to enhance your child's emotional understanding is an easy way to incorporate skill-building into your daily routine.

As you read the story, exaggerate your facial expressions to show the characters' emotions.

This will help your child connect the emotion to the facial expression.

Utilizing media and stories is another powerful technique to enhance emotional learning. Select books, shows, or movies that are age-appropriate and rich in emotional content. As you read or watch together, pause to discuss the characters' emotions and motivations. Ask questions like, "How do you think she feels right now?" or "What do you think he wants to do?" This helps your child practice identifying emotions and enhances their ability to infer feelings from context, a critical skill in understanding complex social interactions. Connecting these stories to real-life situations can deepen your child's understanding. The lessons become more relatable and impactful by drawing parallels between a character's experiences and theirs.

You create a rich learning environment that supports your child's emotional and social development through these methods—utilizing educational tools, modeling expressive communication, engaging in empathy-building activities, and leveraging media and stories. Each activity is a stepping stone towards greater emotional awareness and empathy, crucial skills that enhance personal relationships and broader social interactions. As you continue to guide and support your child in understanding and expressing emotions, you'll likely find that these lessons enrich your emotional experiences and deepen the bond between you and your child.

Navigating Bullying and Social Exclusion

When you think about your child's school day or their time at the playground, one of your deepest hopes is likely that they will find acceptance and friendship. Yet, for many children, especially those on the autism spectrum, the reality can include encounters with bullying and social exclusion. Recognizing the signs that your child might be experiencing bullying is the first critical step in addressing and mitigating its impact. Unlike their neurotypical peers, autistic children may not always communicate their distress directly. They might not say, "I'm being bullied," but you might notice changes in their behavior, such as increased withdrawal, sudden drops in academic performance, or unexplained injuries. They might also exhibit increased anxiety or resistance about going to school or joining in social activities where they previously participated without hesitation.

As parents and caregivers, it's vital to advocate for your child and intervene effectively if bullying occurs. Start by establishing open lines of communication with your child's teachers and school staff. Make them aware of your concerns and collaborate to monitor situations more closely. Schools often have anti-bullying policies in place, but these need to be actively enforced to be effective. Advocate for specific actions, such as supervised transitions between classes, a buddy system, or regular check-ins with a trusted staff member for your child. It's also helpful to educate the school staff about autism-specific sensitivities and social challenges, as awareness can foster a more supportive and understanding environment.

Empowering your child is equally crucial. Autistic children can benefit from learning assertive communication skills that allow them to stand up for themselves or seek help when needed. Role-playing can be a helpful tool here as well. Practice scenarios with your child where they might need to say "stop," ask for help, or join another group of peers. Teach them safe ways to express that they are uncomfortable or upset. Helping your child identify at least one trusted adult at school with whom they feel comfortable discussing their feelings can also provide them with a safe outlet when they feel threatened.

Building a supportive community around your child can significantly buffer the effects of bullying. This includes fostering connections with understanding peers, engaging with inclusive activities, and possibly connecting with local support groups where families with similar experiences share strategies and offer mutual support. Encourage inclusive activities at school that educate all children about diversity and acceptance, perhaps through presentations, inclusive sports teams, or school clubs that celebrate different abilities. These initiatives not only benefit autistic children but enrich the school community as a whole.

Addressing bullying and social exclusion requires a proactive approach, continuous advocacy, and a supportive network. By recognizing the signs, empowering your child with skills and confidence, advocating for systemic support, and fostering an inclusive community, you create a foundation that not only counters the negativity associated with bullying but also promotes a broader culture of understanding and acceptance. Through these efforts, you ensure that your child experiences a safer, more welcoming environment where they can thrive socially and academically.

Celebrating Social Milestones and Progress

In the tapestry of your child's social development, each small stitch—each tiny moment of connection and understanding—contributes to the broader, beautiful picture of their growth. Recognizing and celebrating these moments, no matter how small, is crucial in bolstering your child's confidence and reinforcing their motivation to engage socially. Think of each little success as a sparkle of light; together, they illuminate the path forward, making the journey less daunting for your child. Successfully saying "hello" to a peer, sharing a toy without prompting, or simply responding during a conversation are all milestones worth celebrating. Acknowledging these achievements makes your child feel valued and understood and encourages them to keep trying, engaging, and growing.

CREATING A SOCIAL PROGRESS JOURNAL

A journal can be a tangible record of your child's social journey, capturing moments of triumph and challenges.

Start by regularly jotting down successes and positive interactions, no matter how minor they might seem.

- Did your child play next to another child today?

- Did they ask someone a question?

- Did they respond to a greeting?

Over time, this journal becomes a place where you and your child can look back and see how far they've come, reminding both of you of the successes achieved and the obstacles overcome.

Involving your child in reflecting on their social growth is another empowering tool. This reflection can be as simple as a casual conversation about what felt good about their daily interactions or what they might want to try differently next time. Encourage older children to write or draw in the progress journal, expressing their feelings and experiences in their own words and pictures. This enhances their self-awareness and makes them an active participant in their social development journey. It helps them understand the value of their efforts and see the direct correlation between their actions and achievements. Setting future goals together, based on their reflections, can further personalize this process, making the goals more meaningful and attainable in their eyes.

Family and community recognition is pivotal in reinforcing your child's social achievements. Sharing your child's successes with loved ones can amplify their sense of accomplishment. Consider setting up a small family celebration for key milestones, like mastering a new social skill or making a new friend. These celebrations don't have to be large or elaborate; even a small, intimate acknowledgment can make your child feel incredibly proud and supported. Extending this recognition to the broader community, perhaps by sharing successes with teachers and peers in appropriate settings, further validates their efforts and integrates their achievements into their wider social world. This broader acknowledgment boosts your child's self-esteem and encourages a supportive and inclusive environment around them.

As you continue to navigate the intricate world of social interactions with your child, remember that every effort, success, and setback is integral to their growth. Celebrating these as they come enhances your child's learning experience and strengthens the bonds between you, your child, and the community around you. It's a journey of many steps, and each step deserves its moment of recognition.

Chapter 4

As we close this chapter on fostering social skills, we reflect on the growth journey—from understanding the basics of social interactions to handling complex social dynamics like bullying. In the next chapter, we will explore the world of education and schooling, offering insights and strategies to ensure your child's learning environment is as supportive and enriching as possible. Here, the focus will shift from social interactions to educational achievements, continuing a holistic approach to supporting your child's development.

Your Voice Matters: Help This Book Reach More Families

Every parent navigating the world of autism needs a guiding hand, a source of comfort, and practical strategies.

The Art and Science of Raising Your Autistic Child was created to be that resource—a blend of compassionate advice and actionable insights designed to make a real difference in your family's daily life.

But this book can only fulfill its mission if it reaches those who need it most.

THAT'S WHERE YOU COME IN.

Your honest review will help other parents and caregivers discover this book and understand how it can support their journey. It also helps me continue improving and providing valuable resources for families like yours.

Leaving a review is a small action with a huge potential to make a difference.

With gratitude,

K.M. Burnham

Chapter 5

Time for School - Strategies for Education and School Success

Imagine the first day of school—not just any first day, but one where your child feels understood, supported, and ready to learn in an environment that suits them. Choosing the right school for your autistic child is akin to selecting the soil in which to plant a garden; the better the soil, the more your child will flourish. This chapter is dedicated to guiding you through the intricate process of finding and settling into the school setting that will best nurture your child's growth academically, socially, and emotionally.

Choosing the Right School: Options and Considerations

Evaluating School Options

When it comes to schooling options for autistic children, there is a variety of possibilities, each with its own set of advantages and challenges.

Public Schools

Public or mainstream schools, with their diverse student populations and wide array of extracurricular activities, offer rich opportunities for social integration. These settings can significantly benefit autistic children who can navigate larger class sizes and adapt to a curriculum that moves at a brisk pace. The exposure to a variety of peers and activities can enhance social skills, foster friendships, and promote a sense of belonging. Some mainstream schools have classrooms dedicated to students with special education needs, while others integrate students into general classrooms with support. Parents must assess whether the pace and structure of a mainstream environment align with their child's needs and coping mechanisms.

Special Education Centers

Special education centers specialize in crafting educational experiences meticulously tailored to each child's unique needs. Focusing on smaller class sizes, these centers ensure that each student receives more personalized attention, which can be pivotal for children who thrive under close guidance. Specialized resources, ranging from adaptive technology to sensory-friendly learning materials, are readily available, enhancing the educational experience and catering to the diverse needs of autistic students.

The staff at these centers are trained in general education and possess specialized training in autism education. This expertise allows them to understand the nuanced needs of autistic children, implement effective teaching strategies, and create a structured yet flexible learning environment that adapts to each student's learning pace and style. Such environments are designed to minimize stress and sensory overload, which can be common barriers to learning for children on the spectrum, providing a supportive and understanding backdrop for educational exploration and growth.

<u>Homeschooling</u>

Homeschooling emerges as a profoundly customizable option for families exploring non-traditional educational routes, providing the flexibility to craft a learning environment and curriculum that aligns precisely with a child's unique needs, interests, and learning pace. This path allows for an individualized approach that can deeply resonate with your child's natural curiosity and preferred learning modalities, potentially making education more engaging and effective for them.

However, embracing homeschooling necessitates a substantial commitment from parents or guardians regarding time and resources. It involves the direct instruction of academic subjects and the planning and structuring of a comprehensive educational experience that may include socialization opportunities, extracurricular activities, and specialized therapies or supports. Parents must be prepared to deliver or outsource various educational and developmental interventions, which can be both rewarding and demanding.

Parents considering homeschooling should also be aware of the legal requirements and educational standards set by their local education authorities. Navigating these regulations to ensure compliance while seeking out community resources, support groups, and educational cooperatives can enrich the homeschooling experience and provide vital social and learning opportunities for the child and the parents.

Montessori Schools

Montessori schools champion unique educational philosophies that prioritize child-led learning, offering environments that can be profoundly more flexible and sensory-friendly—qualities that often align well with the needs of autistic children. Montessori schools are characterized by their emphasis on independence, mixed-age classrooms, and a hands-on learning approach. This model allows students to choose their activities from a range of options, encouraging self-directed exploration within a carefully prepared environment. For autistic children, the Montessori setting can provide a sense of control over their learning, reducing anxiety and fostering engagement. The tactile nature of Montessori materials and the individualized pace of learning can also accommodate sensory sensitivities and varied learning styles, making these schools an attractive option for families.

Waldorf Schools

Waldorf schools, on the other hand, focus on holistic education, integrating academic, artistic, and practical activities. This approach aims to equally nurture a child's intellectual, creative, and practical skills. Waldorf education is deeply rooted in the belief that learning should engage and resonate with the child's developmental stage rather than strictly adhering to academic achievement metrics. For many autistic children, the rhythm and predictability of the Waldorf curriculum, combined with its emphasis on creativity and imagination, can create a nurturing space that supports their growth and well-being. Waldorf schools' reliance on storytelling, arts, and hands-on activities can particularly benefit those who find joy and expression in creative pursuits.

Considerations for School Selection

Selecting the right school involves weighing several factors to ensure the best fit for your child. Start by considering the school's experience with autism. Schools with a strong track record of supporting autistic students will likely be better prepared to address their needs effectively. The availability of specialized resources, such as sensory rooms, speech therapy, and occupational therapy, is also crucial. These resources can significantly enhance your child's learning and development.

Inclusion policies are another critical factor. Schools with a strong, inclusive philosophy are likelier to foster an environment where your child can thrive socially and academically. It's also worth considering the school's approach to behavioral support and its alignment with your values and your child's needs. Each of these factors contributes to creating an environment where your child can feel safe, supported, and capable of learning.

Visiting Potential Schools

When visiting potential schools, your observations and questions can provide deep insights into whether the school will be a good fit for your child. Pay attention to the overall environment; does it seem welcoming and accommodating? Observe the interactions between staff and students—does the staff seem patient and understanding? Are there visible accommodations for students with different needs?

Ask about the student-to-teacher ratio, which can affect how much individual attention each student receives. Inquire about the school's policies on bullying and how they handle behavioral issues. It's also essential to ask specific questions about how the school has supported autistic students in the past and how they plan to support your child. This conversation can reveal the practical measures in place and the school's overall attitude towards inclusion and support for neurodiverse students.

Transitioning to a New School

Moving to a new school can be a significant transition for your child, and planning this transition carefully can make the process smoother. Start by preparing your child well in advance, discussing the changes, and visiting the new school multiple times, if possible, to familiarize them with the new environment. Create a visual story that walks through the daily routine at the new school to help reduce anxiety about the unknown.

Work closely with the new school's staff to create a transition plan that includes strategies for effectively supporting your child's learning and adaptation. This might involve gradual integration into the new setting or the support of a school counselor or aide during the initial weeks.

Choosing the right educational path for your child shapes their growth and future. By carefully considering your options, evaluating potential schools, and thoughtfully planning transitions, you can create a supportive educational journey that respects your child's needs and fosters their potential. As you navigate these decisions, remember that the goal is to find a place where your child does not just cope but thrives, finding joy and success in their educational experiences.

The Role of Teachers and Therapists

Navigating the educational landscape with your child can feel like assembling a complex puzzle where each piece represents a different support your child might need. The educators and therapists who will work closely with your child are key among these pieces. Their expertise, approach, and understanding of autism can significantly influence your child's learning and development. Finding the right professionals is not just about checking qualifications; it's about ensuring they have a heartfelt commitment to supporting your child's unique needs. When selecting educators and therapists, look for individuals with specific training and experience working with autistic children. Their specialized knowledge will enable them to effectively tailor their teaching strategies and therapeutic interventions, ensuring they are appropriate and beneficial for your child. It's also important to consider their communication style and how they engage with children. Educators and therapists who use clear, consistent communication and show patience and understanding are likelier to build a trusting relationship with your child.

The role of multidisciplinary teams in supporting your child's education cannot be overstated. These teams often consist of various specialists, including speech therapists, occupational therapists, behavioral therapists, and sometimes special education teachers. Each professional brings a different skill set that addresses different aspects of your child's development. For example, speech therapists work on communication skills, occupational therapists help improve sensory integration and fine motor skills, and behavioral therapists focus on managing challenging behaviors. The collaborative efforts of these professionals ensure a holistic approach to your child's education, catering to all areas of their development. This teamwork makes it possible to create a comprehensive and cohesive plan that supports your child across different environments, whether at home, in school, or social settings.

Maintaining open, regular communication among all team members is crucial for the effectiveness of this collaborative approach. Regular meetings and updates allow each team member to share insights, discuss progress, and adjust strategies as needed. This ongoing dialogue ensures everyone is on the same page, which is essential for consistently applying strategies across different settings. Consistency is vital in helping your child generalize skills from one environment to another, enhancing their overall learning and adaptation. Moreover, when all professionals involved with your child communicate regularly, it reduces the likelihood of overlapping therapies or contradictory strategies, which can confuse your child and hinder their progress.

Empowering educators and therapists to work effectively with your child involves more than just participating in meetings; it's about actively engaging these professionals in a way that encourages a deep understanding of your child's needs. Share insights about what works best for your child, including their likes, dislikes, effective motivators, and particular stressors. This information can be invaluable in helping educators and therapists tailor their approaches. Additionally, providing resources such as articles, workshops, or access to autism specialists can help these professionals stay informed about the latest research and strategies in autism education. By fostering a supportive, informed environment, you enhance the professionals' ability to cater to your child's needs and build a team invested in your child's success.

As you collaborate with this dedicated team, remember that your role is pivotal. You are the expert on your child and an integral part of this multidisciplinary team. Your insights, observations, and feedback are invaluable in shaping educators' and therapists' approaches and strategies. By working together, you can ensure that your child receives the most effective support possible, paving the way for a successful educational experience that respects their needs and maximizes their potential. This collaborative effort supports your child's current developmental needs and lays a strong foundation for their future growth and learning.

Understanding and Developing Effective IEPs

Creating an Individualized Education Program (IEP) is akin to drafting a personalized roadmap that guides your child's educational journey and supports their social, emotional, and behavioral growth. At its heart, an IEP is a detailed document that outlines tailored educational plans and goals specifically designed to meet the unique needs of a child with disabilities, including autism. Understanding the components of an IEP is crucial. It typically includes the child's current performance levels, specific educational goals, special education supports and services, accommodations, modifications, and metrics for measuring progress. This program is not just administrative paperwork; it is a legally binding document that ensures your child receives the education they are entitled to under the Individuals with Disabilities Education Act (IDEA).

Collaboration in developing an IEP is not just beneficial; it's essential. The process involves you, the educators, the therapists, and often your child, coming together to craft a plan that truly reflects the best for the student. This collaborative approach ensures that the IEP is not just a list of goals but a comprehensive strategy that leverages insights from those who know your child best. Engaging in this team effort allows a more well-rounded understanding of your child's abilities, challenges, and potential. It's about pooling knowledge and expertise to create an academic and personal environment where your child can thrive. During these meetings, your voice as a parent is powerful and necessary. Your insights into your child's needs, what works well at home, and where they struggle are invaluable in shaping an effective IEP.

Setting goals within an IEP is a delicate balance of ambition and attainability. These goals should be SMART—Specific, Measurable, Attainable, Relevant, and Time-bound. For instance, if your child struggles with initiating interaction, a SMART goal could be, "By the end of the first semester, [Your Child's Name] will initiate a verbal greeting with peers in four out of five opportunities, as measured by teacher observations." Such a goal is specific in its expectations, measurable by clear criteria, realistically attainable with the proper supports, relevant to your child's social growth, and time-bound within a specific school term. These goals provide clear direction and measurable benchmarks for success, which are crucial for tracking progress and adjusting teaching strategies and supports as needed.

Preparing for an IEP meeting can seem daunting, and the effort is worth it. With the proper preparation, you can advocate effectively for your child's needs. Gather all relevant documentation about your child's educational and medical history.

This can include:

- Report cards,
- Assessments,
- Teacher notes,
- Social Progress Journal
- Therapist and service provider insights.

A well-organized file of this information at the meeting can help inform the discussion and support your points.

Preparing a list of questions and discussion points beforehand is also helpful. Questions might include asking for:

- Clarification on educational jargon,
- Specifics about how goals will be implemented,
- What will happen if the goal is attained early/not attained,
- The best way to contact the team with questions and concerns.

Additionally, consider what accommodations or resources might benefit your child, such as access to a quiet room or technology aids, and be ready to discuss these. Remember, this meeting is your opportunity to ensure your child's educational plan is tailored to their needs, so your active participation is crucial.

By understanding the components and significance of an IEP, engaging in collaborative planning, setting clear, tailored goals, and preparing effectively for IEP meetings, you empower your child to receive an education that meets their academic needs and supports their overall development. This process is fundamental in paving the way for educational experiences that are about learning and thriving. As you navigate this process, remember that your involvement and advocacy are crucial to shaping an academic path that helps your child reach their full potential.

Advocacy in Action: Being a Champion for Your Child's Needs

Understanding the labyrinth of educational rights and advocacy for your child can sometimes feel like navigating a new city without a map. It's crucial to be informed about the legal frameworks designed to protect the educational rights of children with disabilities, including the Americans with Disabilities Act (ADA) and the Individuals with Disabilities Education Act (IDEA). These laws ensure that children with disabilities have equal access to education and are provided with the necessary accommodations to support their learning and integration. The ADA prohibits discrimination based on disability, which encompasses a broad array of conditions, including autism. IDEA, on the other hand, specifically provides children with disabilities the right to a free appropriate public education (FAPE) in the least restrictive environment (LRE). Understanding these laws empowers you to advocate effectively for your child, ensuring they receive the education and support they are entitled to under the law.

When it comes to advocacy, effective communication with school officials is paramount. It's more than expressing your concerns; it's about fostering a partnership with the educators and administrators who interact with your child daily. Start by clearly identifying your child's unique needs and the exact accommodations that would enhance their learning experience. Be specific, providing examples of situations where support might be necessary. Keeping detailed records is also vital in this process. Document everything from your child's progress, any instances of support provided or denied, and all communications with school staff. These records can be invaluable if you need to escalate your concerns or demonstrate patterns that require attention. If issues are not adequately addressed at the school level, know how to escalate appropriately. This might involve talking to higher-level district administrators, seeking mediation, or, as a last resort, pursuing legal avenues. Each step should be measured and considered, always with your child's best interests at the heart of your actions.

Building alliances within the school community can significantly enhance your advocacy efforts. Teachers, administrators, and other parents can be crucial allies in creating a supportive educational environment. Engaging with these stakeholders through regular communication, participating in school meetings, and volunteering for events can help you build relationships and foster a community that genuinely supports inclusive education. When you have nurtured these relationships, you will often find that you have more support when advocating for specific needs or interventions for your child. These allies can provide support and different perspectives that might enhance your understanding of the school's capabilities and limitations.

To bring these concepts to life, let's explore some stories that highlight successful advocacy efforts. One notable example involves a parent whose child was struggling with sensory overload in a busy classroom environment. The parent researched sensory-friendly strategies and proposed specific changes to the classroom setup, including adding a small sensory corner where her child could retreat when overwhelmed. She presented her proposal with evidence of the strategies' effectiveness and worked collaboratively with the teachers and school administrators to implement them.

Over time, not only did her child's ability to focus and learn in the classroom improve, but the teachers also noted a positive change in the overall classroom environment, benefiting other students as well. This success was a direct result of the parent's proactive approach, her willingness to research and suggest practical solutions, and her effective communication and relationship-building with the school staff.

This underscores the power of informed, empathetic advocacy and its impact on enhancing your child's educational experience. By understanding your rights, communicating effectively, keeping detailed records, building strong community ties, and learning from the experiences of others, you can become a formidable advocate for your child. This advocacy is not just about securing services and accommodations; it's about ensuring that your child's education is as enriching and accessible as possible, paving the way for them to reach their full potential. As you continue to advocate for your child, remember that each small victory contributes to a larger goal—a more inclusive, understanding, and supportive educational landscape for all children with different learning needs.

Incorporating Sensory Tools in Learning Environments

Navigating the sensory world can be a complex and overwhelming experience for many autistic children. Sensory sensitivities vary widely; some children might find certain textures unbearable, while others might feel overwhelmed by bright lights or loud noises. Understanding your child's specific sensory needs is the first step towards creating an educational environment where they can thrive.

Working with an occupational therapist can provide invaluable insights into these needs. These professionals specialize in helping individuals achieve independence in all areas of their lives through the therapeutic use of everyday activities. They can assess your child's sensory responses and recommend practical solutions tailored to their needs. For instance, if your child is sensitive to fluorescent lights, the therapist might suggest using filters to soften the light or providing a hat or visor that your child can wear when needed.

When it comes to choosing sensory tools and aids, there's a variety of options that can be integrated into your child's classroom to enhance their learning experience and mitigate sensory overload. Noise-canceling headphones can be a sanctuary for a child who is sensitive to auditory stimuli, allowing them to focus on work without being overwhelmed by background noise. Utilizing weighted vests or lap pads can deliver soothing bodily feedback to your child, fostering a sense of calm and focus essential for engagement in classroom activities. This tactile support enhances your child's concentration, facilitating a more effective learning experience during lessons. Fidget tools, like stress balls or sensory rings, allow children to manage anxiety through tactile stimulation, keeping their hands busy and their minds focused. These tools help manage sensory sensitivities and support cognitive functions, enhancing your child's ability to process information and engage in learning activities more effectively.

Collaboration with educators is crucial in integrating these sensory tools into your child's daily routine at school. Start by having open and honest discussions with your child's teachers about their sensory needs and how these needs can impact their learning and interactions in the classroom. Educators often appreciate when parents provide insights and suggestions based on what has been effective at home or in therapy sessions. Together, you can explore ways to incorporate sensory tools into the classroom to support your child's learning. For example, if using a weighted lap pad helps your child stay seated and focused during homework time at home, this strategy might also be helpful during desk activities at school. Provide the school with the necessary tools and clear instructions on using them. Regular check-ins with the teacher can help ensure that these tools are used effectively and positively impact your child's school experience.

Monitoring the effectiveness of these sensory tools and making necessary adjustments is an ongoing process. It's essential to regularly assess whether the tools meet your child's needs and adjust as needed. This might involve trying different sensory tools, altering how often or in what contexts the tools are used, or even phasing out tools that are no longer effective as your child develops new coping mechanisms. Regular feedback from teachers, observing your child's behavior at home, and continuous communication with your child's occupational therapist can provide valuable information that helps you gauge the success of the interventions. Adjustments should always be carefully considered, ensuring they align with your child's current needs and educational goals.

By understanding your child's unique sensory needs, utilizing appropriate sensory tools, collaborating closely with educators, and continually adjusting strategies, you create a learning environment that accommodates your child's needs and enhances their ability to participate and succeed in educational activities. This proactive approach ensures that school becomes a place where your child feels supported and capable, paving the way for a more positive and productive academic experience. As you implement these strategies, remember that each minor adjustment can make a significant difference in helping your child navigate their sensory world with confidence and ease.

Transitioning Between School Stages

Navigating the shifts between different educational stages can be a pivotal experience for your child, filled with opportunities and challenges. Whether the transition from elementary to middle school or high school to post-secondary options, each phase requires careful planning and support to ensure a smooth and successful transition. Early planning is crucial as it allows you to gather resources, coordinate with educators, and mentally prepare your child for the upcoming changes. Start discussing these transitions well in advance, gradually introducing your child to the idea and discussing what the new stage might look like. This might include visiting the new school or program together, meeting future teachers, or reviewing the new schedule. Such preparations can help demystify the changes for your child, reducing anxiety and building excitement for the new opportunities ahead.

Adjusting the Individualized Education Program (IEP) to match your child's evolving needs as they progress through educational stages is essential. As your child grows, their needs, strengths, and challenges can change, and their IEP should reflect these developments. This might mean setting new goals, introducing different accommodations, or scaling back services that are no longer needed. For example, a child who needed substantial support in elementary school might have gained skills for more independence in middle school. Conversely, new challenges might emerge that require additional support. Regular review meetings with the IEP team provide a platform to assess these needs and make necessary adjustments. It's a dynamic process that requires your active participation and advocacy to ensure that the IEP continues to serve your child's best interests.

Supporting your child's emotional and social adaptation during these transitions is as vital as addressing academic changes. Changes in routine and environment can be unsettling, and your child may need extra support to navigate these waters. If possible, facilitate connections with future classmates by arranging meet-ups or play dates before the transition. Discuss your child's worries about the new stage and brainstorm solutions together. Also, maintain open lines of communication with new teachers and staff, sharing insights about what strategies have helped your child in the past and what might be needed in the new setting. This proactive communication can help ensure the new team is prepared to support your child's social and emotional needs from day one.

Exploring post-secondary options is an exciting part of the transition as your child moves beyond high school. Today, there are more opportunities than ever for autistic individuals, ranging from traditional university programs to vocational training and community integration programs. Each option offers unique benefits, and the right choice will depend on your child's interests, strengths, and support needs. We explore these options more in-depth in chapter eight.

As this chapter ends, remember that each transition your child faces is a step towards new growth and opportunities. By planning early, adjusting education plans, supporting emotional and social needs, and carefully evaluating post-secondary options, you equip your child to navigate these transitions successfully. Each stage brings challenges and achievements, and with the proper support, your child can thrive and move confidently toward a fulfilling future.

In the next chapter, we will delve into the world of holistic approaches to therapy and wellness, exploring how integrating various therapeutic strategies can further support your child's development and overall well-being. As we continue this exploration, remember that each element of support we discuss adds another layer to your child's robust foundation, helping them build a resilient and joyful life.

Chapter 6

Comprehensive Care - Holistic Approaches to Therapy and Wellness

Imagine standing in a garden where each path unfolds to reveal a unique landscape, each designed to engage and heal in its own unique way. This is akin to navigating the diverse world of therapies available for autistic children. Each therapy, like each path in the garden, offers its own form of nurture and growth, tailored to meet your child's distinct needs. This chapter delves into the spectrum of therapeutic options, from the structured realms of behavioral interventions to the expressive arenas of art and drama therapy. Here, you'll learn about the array of therapies and how to discern which path will best support your child's unique journey toward growth and well-being.

Overview of Available Therapies: From ABA to Art Therapy

The landscape of autism therapies is rich and varied, offering numerous approaches, from traditional to holistic, that cater to the diverse needs of children on the spectrum. One conventional method is Applied Behavior Analysis (ABA), a therapy focused on improving specific behaviors through reinforcement strategies. While ABA was once thought of as a gold standard in autism therapies and has been effective for many, it has also faced significant criticism due to its rigid structure and potential for stress on the child. On the other end of the spectrum are creative therapies like art and drama therapy, which offer more flexibility and focus on emotional expression and social skills through creative engagement. These therapies do not seek to change behavior but to understand and develop it through more holistic, child-centered approaches. A more detailed listing of complementary and traditional therapies with descriptions, potential benefits, and cautions is included in the apendix.

Choosing the right therapy for your child involves a blend of intuition and information. Start by considering your child's interests: does your child revel in the quiet focus of painting, or do they find joy in the animated storytelling of drama? The therapy that best aligns with their interests is likely to be the most effective, as it will engage them personally and joyfully. Responsiveness to previous therapies can also guide your decisions. If a particular approach has resonated well with your child in the past, therapies with similar dynamics might also be effective.

Which therapy is suitable for my child?

Here's a short list of possible considerations to guide your evaluation of the available therapies:

Child's Interest: Does the therapy align with what naturally engages and motivates your child?

Past Responsiveness: Has your child shown positive responses to similar forms of therapy?

Therapy Philosophy: Does the therapy's approach resonate with your family's values and goals for your child?

Flexibility and Adaptability: Is the therapy adaptable to your child's changing needs?

Evidence of Efficacy: Is there substantial evidence supporting the effectiveness of the therapy for children with similar needs?

Integrating different therapeutic approaches can often provide comprehensive benefits, addressing multiple aspects of your child's development. For instance, combining a structured technique to develop communication skills with creative outlets to enhance emotional expression can lead to more balanced growth. When integrating therapies, it's crucial to ensure they are harmoniously aligned, complementing rather than contradicting each other. Consulting with professionals who can guide the integration process is essential, ensuring that combined therapies meet your child's needs effectively.

Professional guidance is invaluable in navigating the complex world of autism therapies. A qualified therapist can offer insights into the suitability of different therapies based on their experience and understanding of your child's specific challenges and strengths. They can also help assess the progress made through therapy and make necessary adjustments. If a chosen therapy isn't meeting your child's needs, a professional can help understand why and suggest alternatives or modifications. This adaptive approach ensures that the therapy continues to align with your child's developmental path, providing support where it's most needed.

Navigating the diverse therapies available can feel overwhelming, but with the right tools and guidance, you can make informed choices that pave a path of growth and discovery for your child. Like choosing the right path in a garden, selecting the right therapy involves understanding the landscape, knowing your child's walking style, and sometimes consulting those who know the paths well. With each step forward, you gain more insight into what helps your child thrive, building a therapy experience that is as enriching as it is effective.

The Role of Diet and Nutrition

When you think about the building blocks of a healthy life for your autistic child, diet and nutrition play an integral role, much like the foundation of a house. What we put into our bodies can profoundly affect our feelings and behavior. Understanding how certain foods impact behavior and symptoms in your child is the first step in crafting a dietary plan that supports your child's well-being.

There is no "one size fits all" diet for an autistic child. For instance, some autistic children may have sensitivities to gluten, found in wheat and other grains, or casein, which is a protein in dairy products. These sensitivities can manifest in various ways, from gastrointestinal discomfort to behavioral changes such as increased irritability or hyperactivity. Similarly, sugars and artificial additives in many processed foods can exacerbate hyperactivity and attention issues in some children. By identifying and understanding how the various foods in your child's diet impact behavior, you can make informed decisions about what foods might be best to include or avoid in your child's diet.

The autism community has seen various dietary interventions that many parents and caregivers swear by. It's important to note that most of the support for the diets mentioned comes anecdotally from caregivers and not from scientific studies. For every success story, there may be cases where there's no effect or where managing the diet's restrictions can cause additional stress for the family. This highlights the need for a blended approach: listen to what science says and watch for what works for your child regardless of the science.

Developing a personalized nutrition plan for your child does not have to be a journey you take alone. Working with dietitians who specialize in autism can provide you with the guidance needed to tailor a diet that considers your child's unique needs, preferences, and any existing food sensitivities or allergies.

QUESTIONS TO ASK A DIETITIAN

- What are the most common nutritional deficiencies in autistic children, and how can we address these in my child's diet?

- How can we balance removing certain foods for behavioral improvement without compromising nutritional value?

- Are there specific supplements you recommend that could support my child's overall health and cognitive function?

- Can you help us create a meal plan that considers my child's sensitivities and our family's lifestyle?

Monitoring and adjusting your child's diet over time is crucial, as their needs may change as they grow and as their response to certain foods may evolve. Keeping a food diary can be an incredibly useful tool in this process. By recording what your child eats and any subsequent behaviors or symptoms, you can start to see patterns that might help pinpoint which foods are beneficial and which might be causing issues. Numerous apps can simplify tracking for busy parents, allowing you to quickly enter information and share it with your dietitian or doctor. Regular reviews of this diary with your healthcare provider can help refine the diet plan, ensuring it continues to meet your child's needs effectively.

By understanding the impact of diet on autism and carefully managing and tailoring nutrition plans, you can significantly support your child's health and behavior. Like any therapy or intervention, the key is individualization and ongoing adjustment to find what works best for your child, helping them thrive at their fullest potential.

Incorporating Mindfulness and Meditation

Navigating the bustling, often unpredictable world can be particularly challenging for autistic children, who may experience heightened anxiety and struggle with emotional regulation. This is where the gentle practices of mindfulness and meditation can be a soothing balm, offering tools to help you and your child find calm in the chaos. Understanding the basic principles of mindfulness—staying present in the moment without judgment—can transform daily challenges into opportunities for growth and connection. Similarly, meditation provides a structured way to quiet the mind, making it easier to manage overwhelming emotions and improve focus.

For autistic children, mindfulness exercises can be adapted to fit their needs and capabilities. Simple activities like mindful breathing, where you guide your child to focus on the sensation of air entering and leaving their body, can significantly reduce anxiety and improve their ability to concentrate. Sensory walks, another engaging exercise, involve taking a walk and encouraging your child to notice and describe the sensory experiences around them—like the sound of leaves crunching underfoot or the feel of a gentle breeze. This enhances their sensory integration skills and promotes mindfulness by anchoring them in the sensory details of the present moment. Guided imagery can be particularly effective before transitions or during moments of distress; guiding your child through a visualization of a peaceful place can provide a mental refuge when the outside world feels overwhelming.

If your child struggles with visualization, it's essential to understand that this is a normal variation in how people think. The ability to conjure images in the mind's eye, known as aphantasia, varies widely among individuals. Some people have vivid mental imagery, while others may not visualize at all. This spectrum of visual imagination means that alternative strategies can be equally effective for those who find it difficult to visualize. Encouraging your child to describe scenes, feelings, or experiences in words or drawings rather than trying to force mental images can be a valuable adaptation. This approach allows them to engage in mindfulness and meditation practices in a way that honors their unique neurodiversity profile. By fostering a flexible and inclusive approach to these practices, you ensure every child can participate and benefit from mindfulness, regardless of their innate visual processing style.

Integrating these mindfulness practices into your child's daily routine ensures they become a natural part of their lifestyle rather than an occasional exercise. Regular practice helps these techniques become more effective as your child learns to turn to them instinctively when they start to feel overwhelmed. It's about weaving mindfulness into the fabric of daily life so that it becomes as habitual as brushing their teeth.

DAILY APPLICATION

Applying mindfulness in daily life does not have to take a lot of time. Here are some quick ways to incorporate mindfulness into your child's day:

- Starting each day with a minute of deep breathing together.

- Using sensory walks as a way to decompress after school.

- Eating a snack together and taking turns describing the taste and texture.

The benefits of mindfulness extend beyond your child; they can also be profoundly transformative for you. Embracing mindfulness can help reduce the stress that often comes with parenting, enhancing your emotional resilience. Daily mindfulness practices, like a few minutes of meditation or deep breathing exercises, can help maintain your well-being. Having quick, go-to mindfulness exercises can be invaluable when stress or frustration flare up.

By integrating mindfulness and meditation into your family's routine, you're equipping your child with tools to manage their emotions and enhance their focus. You're also fostering a home environment where calm and presence are valued. This shared commitment to mindfulness practices strengthens your connection, supporting each other in navigating the complexities of life with clarity and calm.

A SIMPLE GROUNDING EXERCISE

This exercise can swiftly bring your focus back to the present, helping manage immediate feelings of anxiety or overwhelm. As you move through the exercise, count and name each item out loud or in your head.

5 - Identify five things you can *see*,

4 - Identify four things you can *touch*,

3 - Identify three things you can *hear*,

2 - Identify two things you can *smell*,

1 - Identify one thing you can *taste*.

The Real-Life Impact of Mindfulness

When my youngest daughter was in middle school, she experienced high levels of frustration during class that would cause her to become overwhelmed and experience a meltdown. This disrupted the entire class, and she felt embarrassed afterward. I had been using three mindful breaths for years when I was feeling frustrated, so I decided it was time to try to teach her the same technique.

I started small, teaching her how to take three deep breaths right before bed to relax her body. As the days progressed, I talked to her about the different times that this could be helpful for her. We also practiced using the three breaths at home when she was starting to have a meltdown.

After many months of spending the evenings before bed teaching her to take these three mindful breaths, she began to ask her teachers, unprompted, for the space to breathe. This transformed not only her experience at school but also that of her classmates and teachers.

The Benefits of Music and Art in Emotional Expression

Imagine a space where colors, shapes, sounds, and textures become languages through which emotions, often trapped deep within, find their expression. This is the essence of music and art therapy, powerful modalities that open new avenues for autistic children to communicate their innermost feelings and thoughts. Unlike traditional therapies that may focus more on verbal communication and behavioral corrections, music and art therapy plunge into the rich depths of emotional expression, offering your child a stage to showcase their individuality without the barriers of conventional language.

Music therapy harnesses melodies, rhythms, and harmonies, creating a symphonic avenue for emotional and social interaction. Music's structured yet flexible nature allows children to engage at their own pace, whether by playing simple percussion instruments, singing along to familiar songs, or just listening and moving to music. This form of therapy not only supports emotional expression but also aids in developing motor skills and coordination. Similarly, art therapy provides a canvas for your child's emotions, where the strokes of a paintbrush or the shaping of clay can articulate feelings that words might not capture. The tactile experience of handling art materials can be particularly therapeutic for children who may be sensory seekers, providing a soothing outlet for their energy and emotions.

DAILY APPLICATION

Create a space at home for creative activities to make the therapeutic benefits integral to daily life.

- Designate a corner of a room or a part of your living area as the creative zone.

- Equip it with accessible and appealing materials, such as non-toxic paints, wide brushes, crayons, safe musical instruments like a keyboard or a small drum, and plenty of paper.

Ensure this space is inviting and organized. It needs to be a place where your child feels motivated to create whenever inspiration strikes.

This setup makes engaging in music and art convenient and signals to your child that their emotional expression through these mediums is valued and encouraged.

While professional therapist-led sessions in music and art offer structured learning and therapeutic benefits, extending these activities into the home setting can significantly amplify their impact. Therapists can provide guidance on specific techniques and exercises that can be replicated at home, tailored to your child's therapeutic needs and artistic preferences. For instance, a music therapist might suggest rhythm exercises you can practice with your child using simple instruments or kitchen utensils, helping them improve their motor skills and ability to cooperate in a shared activity. Art therapists might recommend specific drawing or painting tasks that focus on expressing different emotions, which you can encourage your child to explore during their personal time in the creative space at home.

Real-Life Impact of Music and Art Therapy

Consider the story of Emily, a seven-year-old autistic girl who struggled with severe anxiety and had difficulty expressing her emotions. Through regular art therapy sessions, she began using clay modeling as a form of expression. Over time, Emily created a series of figures representing different family members, each characterized by distinct features that reflected how she perceived their personalities and emotional connections with them. This breakthrough provided her family with insights into her emotional world and improved Emily's ability to interact with them more meaningfully.

Another excellent example is Liam, a ten-year-old boy who found verbal communication challenging. His music therapist introduced him to a keyboard, and over several months, Liam learned to play simple melodies. Playing music became a tool for him to communicate his mood, playing slow, soft tunes when feeling calm and faster, louder music when feeling agitated. This method provided his parents and therapists with an additional way to understand his emotional state and needs, facilitating better support and interaction.

These examples underscore the transformative power of music and art therapy in enabling emotional expression and enhancing communication. For autistic children, these therapies offer a liberating path to convey their feelings and connect with others, enriching their emotional lives and those around them. As you consider integrating these therapies into your child's care plan, remember that the goal is to provide them with enjoyable, expressive outlets that celebrate their unique perspectives and emotional experiences. Through music and art, your child can navigate their emotions more effectively and share their inner world in vibrant, impactful ways.

Physical Activity and Autism: Tailored Exercise Routines

When you think about the role of physical activity in the life of an autistic child, it's much more than just a way to burn off excess energy. It's a vital tool to enhance motor skills, improve sleep quality, and significantly reduce anxiety. These benefits are crucial for the overall well-being of your child, as regular movement helps to regulate the body's natural rhythms and provides a healthy outlet for stress and excess energy. For instance, engaging in physical activities helps improve coordination and muscle tone, which are often areas of challenge for children on the spectrum. Moreover, the repetitive motions involved in certain activities, like swimming or running, can be inherently soothing, providing a rhythmic focus that can help calm an anxious mind. Better sleep often follows physical exertion, which is particularly beneficial as many autistic children struggle with sleep disturbances. A good night's sleep enhances mood, cognitive function, and overall health, making physical activity an essential part of daily life.

Designing autism-friendly exercise programs requires a thoughtful approach that respects your child's sensory sensitivities, physical capabilities, and personal interests. Start by considering the types of movements your child is naturally drawn to. Do they enjoy the feeling of water, making swimming a potentially engaging activity? Or do they prefer the solid sensation of the ground under their feet, which might make walking or running more enjoyable?

Incorporating sensory-friendly aspects into the exercise routine can also make a significant difference. For example, outdoor activities might be preferable to a noisy gym environment if your child is sensitive to loud noises. Similarly, if they are overwhelmed by the visual stimulation of a crowded space, choosing less populated areas for activities or going at off-peak times can help. The key is to adapt the environment and the activities to fit your child's needs, making physical activity a stress-free and enjoyable part of their day.

Highlighting sports programs and activities that are particularly suitable for autistic children can open up new avenues for physical and social growth. Programs like adaptive yoga offer structured yet flexible environments where children can learn at their own pace, with enough repetition to make the activities predictable but enough variety to keep them engaged. Martial arts, particularly those that emphasize individual progress like Taekwondo, can be beneficial for self-discipline and motor coordination, providing clear routines and expectations. Swimming is another excellent activity, as the sensory experience of water can be incredibly soothing for many autistic children, and the skills learned can enhance confidence and safety. Many communities offer specialized sports programs designed with the needs of autistic children in mind, providing supportive, understanding environments where children can thrive. Engaging with local autism support groups or checking with community centers can help you find these programs, making integrating beneficial physical activities into your child's routine easier.

Encouraging family involvement in physical activities can transform exercise from a routine into a cherished family bonding time. When the whole family participates, it makes the activity more enjoyable for your child and reinforces the importance of a healthy lifestyle for everyone. This shared experience can strengthen family ties, creating shared memories and experiences that enhance family dynamics. Whether it's a weekend family hike, an evening walk after dinner, or a morning yoga session, these activities provide routine touchpoints that bring the family together, fostering a sense of unity and mutual support. Moreover, involving siblings in these activities can help them understand and connect with their autistic brother or sister, deepening their bond through shared experiences.

By incorporating regular physical activity into your child's life, you're not just enhancing their physical health; you're also opening doors to improved emotional well-being, better sleep, and enriched family and social relationships. Tailoring exercise routines to meet the unique needs of your autistic child can provide them with a powerful tool for navigating both their internal and external worlds, offering a pathway to greater health, happiness, and connection. As you explore and integrate these physical activities, observe how each one impacts your child, and adjust as needed to ensure that each step, swim, or stretch brings them joy and comfort, paving the way for a healthier, more balanced life.

Holistic Success Stories

Diving into the personal stories of families who have navigated the complexities of autism with holistic approaches provides both inspiration and practical insights that can light your path. Each story is a testament to the power of tailored therapies and unwavering parental dedication.

Take, for instance, the story of Clara, a young girl whose world was transformed through a blend of sensory integration therapy and a carefully structured gluten-free diet. Her parents noticed early on that Clara was particularly sensitive to tactile inputs and certain food textures, which often led to distress and disconnection. After consulting with a team of occupational therapists and a nutritionist specializing in autism, they introduced sensory integration sessions that were carefully timed after meals to ensure Clara was at her most receptive. The dietary adjustments included eliminating gluten, which her parents and specialists suspected might be exacerbating her sensory sensitivities.

Over the months, Clara began to show remarkable improvements in her ability to engage with her environment and communicate her needs more clearly, demonstrating less anxiety around mealtimes and new textures. This case beautifully illustrates how combining dietary management with therapy tailored to sensory needs can create an environment where a child can thrive more fully.

Another compelling story is that of Samuel, whose journey underscores the value of integrating music therapy with behavioral techniques. Diagnosed with autism at an early age, Samuel struggled with verbal expression and often became frustrated when unable to communicate his thoughts and feelings. His breakthrough came when his therapist introduced a program that combined music therapy with a positive reinforcement system. Music sessions gave Samuel a non-verbal outlet for his emotions, using instruments and rhythms to express what words could not. Meanwhile, each successful communication attempt during these sessions was met with tangible rewards reinforcing his efforts and encouraging further interaction. Over time, Samuel's ability to express himself improved significantly, highlighting how creative therapies, combined with behavioral strategies, can enhance communication and emotional expression.

Several key lessons emerge from these stories for any parent navigating similar challenges. First, the importance of a personalized approach cannot be overstated. What works for one child may not work for another, and the success of an intervention can often depend on how well it is tailored to the individual's specific needs and preferences. Second, the integration of multiple therapeutic approaches frequently yields the best outcomes. A multidisciplinary approach that considers all aspects of a child's development can address complex needs more effectively than any single therapy. Finally, professional guidance is crucial in navigating this complex landscape. Specialists who understand the nuances of autism can provide invaluable support and insights, helping to adjust and refine strategies as your child grows and their needs evolve.

Experts in the field echo these sentiments, emphasizing the importance of a holistic, integrated approach to autism therapy. They advocate for continuous assessment and flexibility in therapy plans, ensuring that the most effective interventions meet each child's evolving needs. These professionals contribute their expertise and provide a support system for families, guiding them through the challenges and celebrating the milestones along the way.

As we wrap up this exploration of holistic success stories, we carry the powerful lessons and inspiring breakthroughs that mark each journey. They remind us that in the world of autism, where challenges and victories intertwine, the path to success is paved with patience, understanding, and the courage to tailor the journey to meet the unique needs of your child.

Now, we turn towards an essential, yet frequently undervalued, element in nurturing an autistic child: the holistic well-being of the caregiver and the family unit. This transition underscores the necessity of embracing not just your child's developmental trajectory but also the emotional, psychological, and physical health of those providing care. It is a reminder that the caregiving environment's resilience, strength, and stability directly influence your child's progress and well-being. The upcoming sections will delve into strategies for caregiver self-care, fostering a supportive family ecosystem, and building a resilient, nurturing environment that benefits all members. This holistic approach not only enhances the quality of life for your child but also fortifies the family as a whole, ensuring that everyone's needs are met with compassion, understanding, and effective support.

Chapter 7
Taking Care of You - Parental and Family Well-Being

Imagine you're sitting in a quiet room, the soft hum of the world outside barely whispering through the walls. Here, in this moment, you're not just a caregiver; you're a person with needs, dreams, and a right to rest. This chapter delves into a crucial aspect of parenting often overshadowed by the day-to-day demands of raising an autistic child: your well-being. It's a gentle reminder that taking care of yourself is not a luxury—it's essential. Like securing your oxygen mask before assisting others, self-care enables you to be the best parent you can be. Here, we explore practical, achievable ways to incorporate self-care into your life, ensuring you have the energy, patience, and emotional resilience to navigate both the joys and challenges of parenting.

Self-Care Strategies for Parents: Finding Time and Space

Prioritizing self-care is fundamental, not just for your well-being but also for your ability to effectively care for your child. It's easy to dismiss self-care as secondary, especially when your child needs so much attention and support. However, neglecting your needs can lead to burnout, resentment, and exhaustion—emotions that, if left unchecked, can affect the whole family's dynamics. Think of self-care as the foundation of a strong house; without it, the entire structure risks collapse.

Integrating self-care into your daily routine might sound impossible, but it can be as simple as dedicating a few minutes each day to activities that replenish your spirit. Start small. It could be three minutes of morning meditation, a single chapter of a book at lunch, or a short walk after dinner. The key is consistency. These moments of pause are vital breaths of fresh air, clearings in the forest of your responsibilities. Mindfulness practices, such as deep breathing or focusing on a single sensory input, can be particularly effective in managing stress. They anchor you in the present, helping diffuse the anxiety and overwhelm often accompanying parenting.

Creating a personal space in your home for downtime is equally important. This doesn't need to be an entire room; a small corner where you can sit undisturbed, perhaps with a comfortable chair or cushion on the floor, a soft throw, and a stack of your favorite books, can become your sanctuary. This personal space is your retreat, a physical representation of taking a step back, where you can breathe, gather your thoughts, and center yourself before stepping back into the fray.

Effective time management is crucial in making room for these self-care practices. It involves realistic planning— acknowledging what you can do versus what you want to do. Setting daily goals can help you manage your time efficiently, but these goals need to be achievable to avoid the trap of overcommitment. Learn to delegate tasks when possible, and remember, it's okay to say no. Protecting your time is not selfish; it's necessary to maintain your health and well-being.

As you explore these strategies, remember that self-care is not a one-size-fits-all prescription. It's deeply personal, shaped by your unique needs, responsibilities, and joys. By making self-care a non-negotiable part of your routine, you're enhancing your well-being and modeling healthy habits for your family. It's a journey of small steps, each leading you to a more balanced, fulfilling life as a parent and individual.

TIME MANAGEMENT EXERCISE:

REFLECT AND PRIORITIZE

Keep a diary of how you spend your time for one week.

Write down how you spend your time each day. For example:

Monday

- 6 a.m., woke up and scrolled on social for 10 minutes.

- 6:30 a.m. - 7:30 a.m., got ready for work and made breakfast.

- 7:30 a.m. - 8 a.m., watched the news.

Review your activities at the end of each day and categorize them into 'must do,' 'needs to do,' and 'want to do.'

At the end of the week, review your entries.

You might find that time slips away in unexpected ways, in tasks that could be delegated or streamlined. Use this insight to make adjustments, ensuring that each day includes tasks you must do and activities you want to do—those that nourish your spirit.

Mental Health Resources for Families

Navigating the complexities of raising an autistic child can sometimes feel like managing a delicate ecosystem. Every element needs attention, and the whole's health often depends on its parts' well-being. That's why accessing robust mental health resources is crucial for your child and every family member. From counseling services tailored to special needs families to innovative mental health apps and emergency hotlines, a wealth of resources is available to support you. Counseling services, for instance, can provide a safe space to explore the challenges and stresses unique to your family's situation. These professionals are trained to help you develop strategies to cope with daily stresses and offer therapeutic interventions to benefit the entire family dynamic.

Finding the right mental health professional is a journey of its own. It starts with understanding the specific needs of your family. For instance, some families might benefit from therapists who specialize in autism and can offer guidance specific to the spectrum. In contrast, others might benefit from a therapist skilled in neurodiverse family dynamics. When you seek professional help, expect the first few sessions to be about building rapport and setting the groundwork for future work. During these initial meetings, assessing whether the therapist's approach aligns with your family's needs and values is essential. Ask questions about their experience with autism, their therapeutic approach, and expected outcomes. If something doesn't feel right, seeking a second opinion is okay. Finding a good fit can make a significant difference in the effectiveness of the therapy.

Several therapeutic approaches have proven beneficial for families dealing with autism. Cognitive-behavioral therapy (CBT), for instance, is effective in addressing anxiety and depression, which can be common in parents of autistic children. It focuses on changing thought patterns to improve emotional regulation and develop effective coping strategies. Family systems therapy is another approach that can be incredibly beneficial, as it views the family as an interconnected system where changes in one part affect the whole. This type of therapy can help improve communication between family members, resolve conflicts, and understand each member's role in the family dynamics.

In addition to therapy, many self-help and educational materials can offer further support. Books like "The Loving Push" by Temple Grandin and Debra Moore delve into strategies that help parents encourage independence in their autistic children. Websites like Autistic Self Advocacy Network provide resources and articles to help you understand the spectrum more deeply. Additionally, online forums and webinars can offer community support and practical advice that can be accessed from the comfort of your home. These resources can be invaluable in providing day-to-day support and ensuring you are informed and empowered in your parenting journey.

Navigating mental health needs is a continuous process of adaptation and learning involving an array of resources, from personal therapy to community support. Each step to bolster your family's mental health is a step towards a more resilient, understanding, and supportive family environment. As you use these resources, remember that the goal is not just to manage challenges but to build a foundation of understanding and support that will benefit your entire family for years to come.

Family Therapy: When and How It Can Help

Navigating the waves of family life when raising an autistic child can sometimes feel like steering through a storm without a compass. During these times, family therapy can serve as a guiding light, offering strategies and insights that help calm the waters for everyone aboard. Recognizing when to seek family therapy is critical. It can be particularly beneficial during significant transitions such as changes in schooling, shifts in family dynamics, or following the initial autism diagnosis. These periods can strain even the strongest bonds, and a family therapist specializes in fortifying these connections, ensuring that each family member's voice is heard and valued.

Family therapy aims to foster a healthier, more supportive family environment, which is essential for the well-being of all members, especially your autistic child. The goals of this therapeutic approach often include enhancing communication between family members, resolving conflicts that arise from differing expectations, and helping the family adjust to the unique needs of the autistic child. For instance, a common challenge might be balancing the attention between siblings, where a non-autistic sibling might feel overshadowed by the more pressing needs of their autistic brother or sister. Family therapy can open up a dialogue that helps to redistribute family roles and responsibilities more equitably, ensuring that no one feels left out or overburdened.

Chapter 7

Selecting the right therapist is crucial to the success of family therapy. It's important to find a professional with the credentials, experience, and understanding necessary to navigate the complexities of autism. Look for a therapist who has a background in dealing with neurodiverse families. They should be someone who resonates with your family's values and approaches challenges with empathy and innovative strategies. During your initial meetings, observe how the therapist interacts with all family members and whether their approach feels respectful and inclusive. It's often a good sign if they encourage open communication and foster a sense of safety where each family member feels comfortable expressing their thoughts and feelings.

Maximizing the benefits of family therapy involves more than just showing up to sessions. Active participation from each family member is essential. This means everyone is engaged, ready to explore the dynamics at play, and open to implementing the strategies discussed during therapy. Setting clear goals at the outset can be incredibly helpful. These goals might include changes you hope to see in family interactions or emotional responses to everyday challenges. The therapist can help you outline these objectives and develop a plan to achieve them, providing a clear framework for the therapy process. Additionally, integrating the techniques and communication styles learned in therapy into your daily interactions can lead to lasting change. It's about taking those insights and tools from the therapy sessions and weaving them into the fabric of your daily life, which reinforces new behaviors and ways of relating to one another.

Family therapy is not just about resolving conflicts or addressing challenges—it's also a pathway to deeper understanding and stronger connections within your family. As you learn and grow together through this process, you not only enhance your family's ability to support each other but also create a nurturing environment where every member, especially your autistic child, can thrive.

Building and Leveraging Support Networks

Creating a support network might seem like another task on an overflowing list. However, think of it as weaving a safety net that not only catches you when you fall but also lifts you higher than you could ever reach on your own. It's about surrounding yourself with people and resources that understand the specific trials and triumphs of raising an autistic child. This network can include extended family and friends who get it, community groups, and even online forums where you can share, learn, and lean on each other. Identifying these support systems means looking around and recognizing who makes you feel supported, understood, and less alone.

Family and friends can be invaluable, but their support is often most beneficial when they truly understand your situation. It might help to have open conversations about your child's needs and what kind of support feels helpful. Sometimes, it's about practical help, like taking care of your child for a couple of hours so you can rest. Other times, it's about having someone who listens without judgment when you need to vent. Encouraging family and friends to join you at therapy sessions or autism workshops can also increase their understanding and ability to support you effectively.

Community resources often offer a treasure trove of support, from local autism support chapters to parent-led workshops.

These resources can connect you with families on similar paths, providing opportunities to share strategies and support. Local chapters often organize events and meet-ups, which can be great for you and your child to find new friends who understand your daily life. Additionally, many communities have parent training programs that can provide you with tools and strategies that have been effective for others in your area.

The online world offers another layer of connectivity, with countless forums, social media groups, and websites dedicated to autism support. These platforms can provide advice at your fingertips, often from people who have faced similar challenges and found workable solutions. However, tread carefully in the digital space. Choose online communities that are well-moderated and known for being supportive and positive. It's essential to protect yourself from misinformation and negative interactions, which, unfortunately, are also part of the online world. Engaging positively means asking questions, sharing experiences, and using what you learn to better your family's journey. While online advice can be helpful, it should never replace professional guidance.

Network Building Activities: Autism Awareness Events

Consider participating in or even organizing autism awareness events in your community. These events raise awareness and build community ties. Activities could include fun runs, information booths, or art exhibitions featuring work by autistic artists. These events can boost your local network by connecting you with educators, therapists, and other parents. It's also a chance for the broader community to learn about autism, which can foster a more inclusive environment for your child.

Building and leveraging your support network is about creating a community that uplifts and supports each other. It's about finding those connections that provide help and hope. As you strengthen your network, you enhance your capacity to manage and thrive, contributing to a supportive, understanding, and inclusive community for your child.

Sibling Workshops and Support Groups

Navigating family life when one of your children is on the autism spectrum involves more than just understanding and supporting your autistic child; it's also about nurturing the bonds between siblings. Sibling workshops and support groups play a crucial role in this dynamic. They provide a space where siblings can learn about autism, share their experiences, and develop coping strategies in a supportive environment. These programs are essential because they help normalize the family situation and explain behaviors that might otherwise be misunderstood. Siblings often benefit from realizing they are not alone in their experiences, and these groups can help them see that other families face similar challenges. This understanding can foster patience and empathy among siblings, strengthening the family unit.

Finding the right support group or workshop for siblings can vary greatly depending on where you live and your family's specific needs. Start by checking with local autism advocacy organizations—many offer sibling programs. Hospitals and therapy centers are also good resources, as they often host support groups that cater to various age groups. Websites dedicated to autism support frequently have forums or listings for sibling workshops and virtual meet-ups that address the needs of different age groups. When selecting a group, consider the age-appropriateness and the program's focus to ensure it aligns with your children's needs and their ability to understand and engage with the material presented.

CREATING YOUR OWN SIBLING WORKSHOP

To start, brainstorm the topics that would most benefit your children and what activities will be most useful for exploring them.

Potential Topics: understanding sensory issues, communicating effectively with their sibling, and handling public reactions to autism-related behaviors.

Potential Activities: role-playing, discussion sessions, arts and crafts, and expressing feelings about an autistic sibling.

Inviting a professional, such as a child psychologist or a behavioral therapist, can lend expertise and depth to the discussions. Remember, the goal is to empower siblings with knowledge and skills, making them feel more confident and proactive in their relationships.

Strong sibling relationships are vital and can be nurtured through shared activities that cater to the interests of the autistic child and their siblings. Choose activities that encourage cooperation rather than competition, such as building a model, creating a family scrapbook, or working together on a puzzle. These activities provide fun and relaxed bonding opportunities and allow siblings to engage with each other in a structured way that minimizes stress and conflict. It's important during these activities to monitor interactions and provide guidance as needed. This ensures that all children feel included and valued, reinforcing the bonds between them.

Encouraging siblings to express their thoughts and feelings about having an autistic brother or sister is equally important. Sometimes, siblings need reassurance that their feelings are normal and valid. Regular family meetings where everyone, including siblings, can discuss their feelings, frustrations, and joys can be very beneficial. This open dialogue helps to prevent feelings of resentment or isolation that siblings may experience. It also allows parents to address concerns and support their children in coping with their challenges.

Fostering these relationships and setting up supportive structures like workshops and groups not only supports your autistic child but also nurtures a family environment where all members feel understood, supported, and connected. This holistic approach to family dynamics is crucial for everyone's well-being and ensures that each family member can thrive individually and together.

Dealing with Burnout: Signs and Solutions

In the relentless ballet of parenting, especially under the unique pressures that come with raising an autistic child, burnout lurks as an all-too-common shadow. It's about more than feeling tired. Burnout can manifest as a profound exhaustion that permeates your physical, emotional, and mental states, leaving you feeling detached, ineffective, and utterly drained. Recognizing the signs early can be a game-changer. Physical symptoms like chronic fatigue, insomnia, or frequent headaches can be clues, as well as emotional signs such as irritability, sadness, or a feeling of disconnect from your loved ones. If you find yourself less interested in activities you once enjoyed or notice that your patience wears thin more quickly, these could be critical signals that your well-being needs attention.

Proactive measures are crucial to staving off burnout. Setting boundaries is perhaps one of the most challenging yet vital strategies. It involves acknowledging and communicating your limits—how much time and energy you can devote to various demands before it impairs your well-being. Learning to say no, or not now, is not a sign of weakness; it's a crucial skill that protects your energy reserves and keeps resentment at bay. Striking a healthy balance between work, parenting, and personal time isn't about achieving a perfect split but ensuring that all areas receive adequate attention so that one doesn't overwhelmingly consume the others.

Recovery from burnout requires a conscious effort to rekindle your spirit and reconnect with the joys of parenting and life. Techniques for emotional rejuvenation vary widely, but they often involve reconnecting with your interests and passions.

This might mean picking up a hobby you've set aside, spending time in nature, or simply allowing yourself a "do nothing" afternoon with a good book or a favorite movie. These activities aren't indulgent—they're necessary for restoring your emotional energy. Additionally, consider practices like journaling or meditation, which can help you process your feelings and regain a sense of peace and control.

Supporting each other in a parental partnership can significantly buffer the stresses that lead to burnout. This support can look like alternating responsibilities with childcare, providing each other with time off to decompress, or simply offering a listening ear without judgment. Regular, open communication about each other's well-being can prevent misunderstandings and ensure both partners feel supported and valued. When parenting solo, leaning on a trusted friend, family member, or support group can provide similar relief and understanding.

Maintaining a reflective journal can help deepen your understanding of your burnout triggers and effective coping strategies. Regular entries about your day-to-day experiences and feelings can help you identify patterns that lead to stress and discover activities that most effectively replenish your energy. This practice not only aids in immediate stress relief but also enhances your long-term resilience by building a personalized toolkit of strategies that work for you.

REFLECTIVE JOURNALING PROMPT

Reflect on a moment today when you felt stressed or burnt out.

- What was happening that made you feel that way?

- What did you do to deal with it?

Write down what worked well and what you might want to try differently tomorrow.

In navigating these strategies, the goal is not to eliminate stress entirely—that's an unrealistic expectation for any parent, let alone when raising an autistic child. Instead, it's about managing stress so that it doesn't accumulate to the point of burnout. It's about recognizing the early signs of emotional and physical exhaustion and taking proactive steps to address them. By setting boundaries, engaging in rejuvenating activities, and fostering supportive relationships, you can protect your well-being, ensuring you have the energy and spirit to enjoy the rewarding journey of raising your child.

As this chapter closes, we prepare to delve into the final discussions of our guide. This next chapter aims to equip you with the knowledge and tools to handle future changes smoothly, ensuring that as your child grows, so too does your ability to support them effectively.

Chapter 8
Looking Ahead - Preparing for Adolescence and Adulthood

Just like the first signs of spring hint at the changing seasons, subtle shifts in your child's behavior signal the arrival of adolescence, marking the start of a new chapter in their life. This phase, rich with growth and transformation, can feel like navigating a rapidly changing landscape without a map. Yet, here lies an opportunity to deepen the bond with your child, guiding them through the physical, emotional, and social evolutions with sensitivity and understanding.

In this chapter, we'll explore the multifaceted changes of puberty and how you can support your child through this critical period, ensuring that the journey through adolescence is approached with informed care and heartfelt connection.

Preparing for Puberty: Changes and Challenges

When should I start thinking about preparing my child for adolescence?

In anticipation of adolescence, forward-thinking and early preparation are vital to navigating the upcoming changes with grace and understanding. Initiating conversations and readiness activities for puberty a minimum of five years ahead is recommended. This strategic early start fosters a gentle, age-appropriate introduction to bodily changes, emotional shifts, and evolving social interactions. By establishing this foundation well in advance, you create a nurturing, open space for your child to navigate these forthcoming transitions, ensuring they feel embraced and well-informed as they embark on this significant phase of their journey.

Understanding Physical Changes

As your child steps into puberty, their body will begin a journey of significant transformation, which can be perplexing and sometimes overwhelming for autistic individuals. They may face challenges with physical changes such as growth spurts, voice changes, and the onset of menstruation or facial hair, which are standard aspects of puberty but can feel particularly intense for those with heightened sensory sensitivities. These physical developments can sometimes amplify sensory discomfort, like an increased sensitivity to clothing textures or personal hygiene products that previously seemed fine. Recognizing and validating these experiences is crucial, as it reassures your child they are not alone in their feelings.

Educating yourself and your child about these changes before they occur can demystify the process and reduce anxiety. Simple, clear explanations about what to expect can be incredibly reassuring. Visual aids like diagrams or age-appropriate books can help make the information more accessible. Remember, each child's receptivity to learning about their changing body will vary, so tailor your approach to fit their comfort level and understanding. For those with more profound sensitivities, consider consulting with a pediatrician or an occupational therapist to explore strategies or products that can alleviate discomfort, such as seamless clothing or unscented hygiene products tailored for sensitive skin.

Addressing Emotional Fluctuations

The hormonal surges during puberty can create an emotional rollercoaster, not just for neurotypical adolescents but even more so for those on the autism spectrum who may already be navigating complex emotional landscapes. These fluctuations can manifest as mood swings, increased irritability, or sudden bouts of anxiety and sadness. It's a time when your empathetic communication and stable presence become their safe harbor in the storm.

Creating a routine with regular check-ins can be a soothing anchor for your child. These moments of connection are opportunities to affirm your unconditional support and love, helping to stabilize their emotional world. Remind them to use their coping mechanisms like deep breathing exercises, sensory breaks, or quiet time in a designated safe space at home where they can retreat when feelings become overwhelming. Encourage them to express their emotions through creative outlets such as drawing, music, or journaling, which can provide a non-verbal pathway for processing complex feelings.

Sexual Education Tailored to Autistic Learners

Navigating the topic of sexual education is critical during this period, as it equips your child with the knowledge they need to understand their body, establish boundaries, and recognize appropriate and inappropriate social behaviors. For autistic learners, sexual education needs to be explicit, concrete, and judgment-free, addressing both safety and social norms.

Finding resources outside the traditional school system might be necessary to ensure the content is accessible for your child's learning style. Organizations specializing in disability education often offer programs and materials designed with neurodiverse learners in mind. These programs not only cover the biological aspects of sex education but also focus on consent, relationships, and self-esteem, all crucial for your child's social and emotional development.

Communication Channels

Open communication about puberty is essential. It helps your child navigate their feelings and changes with confidence rather than confusion. Initiating these conversations might feel overwhelming, but being proactive and transparent can ease the potential awkwardness. Use clear and direct language, and be prepared to repeat information in different ways to ensure understanding. Visual aids, like charts or storyboards, can help illustrate concepts that might be difficult to explain verbally.

Set a tone of openness and non-judgment from the start. Let your child know that no topic is off-limits and that you're there to listen and support, not to judge. Regularly scheduled talks can help make these conversations a normal part of life rather than a series of awkward encounters. This ongoing dialogue prepares them for puberty changes and strengthens your relationship, reinforcing the trust and openness that will support both of you through adolescence and beyond.

Educational Transitions: High School to Higher Education or Work

As your child nears the end of high school, the question of 'what comes next?' begins to loom larger. It's a period filled with potential, packed with decisions about further education and work opportunities. Navigating this transition effectively requires careful planning and a deep understanding of your child's needs and aspirations. Let's explore how you can guide your child through these pivotal years to ensure they embark on a path that meets their educational and career goals and supports their overall development and happiness.

Planning for Post-secondary Education

Exploring options for higher education is like setting out on a vast sea of opportunities. Each institution offers a unique set of programs, supports, and environments, and finding the right fit for your child can profoundly impact their future. Start by considering the spectrum of possibilities: traditional four-year colleges, community colleges, and specialized programs for autistic students. Each option comes with its strengths. Traditional colleges often provide a broad range of courses and the classic college experience but may require strong self-advocacy skills and the ability to navigate a large campus environment. Community colleges offer more flexible learning schedules and smaller class sizes, which might benefit students who thrive in less overwhelming settings. On the other hand, specialized programs are tailored specifically to support neurodiverse students, offering structures that address their unique learning needs and challenges.

When evaluating these options, consider academic supports, such as tutoring, access to learning resources, and accommodations like note-taking services or extended time for assignments and exams. If possible, visit campuses and talk to staff about available support services. Contacting current students or alums from these programs can also provide insider perspectives that are invaluable in making your decision. Remember, the goal is to find a place where your child feels supported and can thrive academically, socially, and personally.

Transition IEPs

As your child prepares to move from high school to what lies beyond, the Individualized Education Program (IEP) transitions into what is known as a Transition IEP. This plan specifically focuses on your child's post-high school goals, covering academic achievement, post-secondary education, and independent living. The development of a Transition IEP should begin by the time your child turns 16, but it's wise to start discussions as early as possible. This plan is a collaborative effort involving you, your child, educators, and possibly other professionals like therapists or counselors.

The Transition IEP should outline realistic steps to help your child achieve their future goals. This includes identifying courses and experiences that support their ambitions, whether attending college, entering the workforce, or living independently. It might also involve connecting with outside agencies offering vocational training or employment opportunities. Effective implementation of this plan requires regular reviews and updates as your child's interests and goals evolve. Your active involvement ensures that the transition process remains aligned with their aspirations and needs, providing a structured yet flexible roadmap to their future.

Workplace Readiness

Preparing for the workforce involves equipping your child with the necessary job skills and the soft skills required to navigate the workplace. Start by identifying their strengths and areas where they might need development. Vocational assessments can be beneficial here, providing insights into potential career paths that align with their skills and interests. Following this, targeted training programs, internships, or part-time jobs can be excellent opportunities for gaining practical experience.

Workplace accommodations are also crucial for supporting autistic individuals in their jobs. These might include a quiet workspace to reduce sensory overload, clear written task instructions, or flexible scheduling. Educating potential employers about these accommodations can foster a more inclusive and supportive work environment. Additionally, role-playing interviews or work scenarios at home can help your child practice responding to different situations they might encounter, building their confidence and preparedness.

Leveraging Vocational Rehabilitation Services

Vocational rehabilitation services offer valuable resources for individuals with disabilities, including autism. They provide support that ranges from job training to education and employment placement. These services are designed to help individuals achieve independence through gainful employment, aligning job opportunities with the individual's capabilities and interests. Engaging with these services early can help set the foundation for a smooth transition from school to the workforce.

To access these services, you'll need to apply through your state's vocational rehabilitation agency. The process typically involves an assessment of your child's needs and capabilities, followed by developing an individualized plan for employment. This plan might include job coaching, help finding and applying for jobs, and ongoing support once employment is obtained. Navigating this system can seem daunting, but the support it offers can be instrumental in helping your child find meaningful employment that aligns with their skills and interests.

As you and your child navigate these educational and vocational waters, remember that each step forward is a step toward greater independence and fulfillment. The choices made during this time can open doors to new opportunities and pave the way for a successful and satisfying adult life.

Vocational Training and Employment Opportunities

Finding the right vocational path for your adolescent can feel like piecing together a puzzle. Each piece represents different aspects of their abilities and interests and, when placed correctly, reveals a clear picture of potential career paths that provide fulfillment and a sense of independence and pride. Assessing these skills and interests is the first crucial step. It starts with observation—pay attention to what activities your child is naturally drawn to. Do they show a keen interest in computers and technology? Are they fascinated by how things work, perhaps showing mechanical inclinations? Or do they have a creative streak that comes alive with colors and designs? Formal assessments, often available through school programs or vocational rehabilitation services, can provide valuable insights. These assessments go beyond surface-level observations to uncover deeper strengths and aptitudes, guiding you toward appropriate vocational training programs that can turn these interests into employable skills.

Job coaching services become invaluable when transitioning from training to actual employment. These coaches work with individuals with disabilities, including autism, to bridge the gap between acquired skills and real-world applications. They help refine these skills and teach job-specific competencies, such as understanding workplace etiquette, managing time effectively, and communicating with coworkers and supervisors. Beyond skill training, job coaches provide support that eases the often intimidating process of entering the workforce. They can accompany your child to the job site, helping them adjust to the new environment and tasks. This support is tailored, sometimes fading gradually as your child gains confidence and independence, ensuring a supported release into their job responsibilities.

Creating a supportive work environment is crucial for the success of autistic individuals in the workforce. As you explore potential employment opportunities, look for inclusive workplaces known for diversity and accommodation policies. These environments often have structures in place to support employees with disabilities, such as sensory-friendly workspaces or flexibility in work hours, which can be crucial for managing stress and sensory overload. Encourage your child to share their needs and advocate for accommodations that will help them perform their best, such as using noise-canceling headphones in noisy areas or having access to a quiet room for breaks. Preparing for scenarios where the work environment may not initially meet all their needs is also important. In such cases, having open dialogues with employers about necessary adjustments can make a significant difference. Empower your child with the skills to communicate their needs effectively or, if needed, step in to facilitate these conversations, ensuring their comfort and productivity at work.

Amidst these practical steps, the stories of autistic individuals flourishing in their careers provide not just inspiration but tangible proof of what is possible with the proper support and opportunities. Consider the story of Jonathan, who discovered a passion for graphic design during a vocational training program. His attention to detail and strong visual skills made him a perfect candidate for this field. With the support of a job coach, Jonathan secured a position at a design firm that values diversity and inclusivity. His employer implemented a few accommodations, like providing written instructions for assignments and allowing him to wear headphones to minimize distractions. Jonathan's success is a testament to the potential that can be unlocked when interests are aligned with vocational training and supported by an understanding workplace. These success stories not only serve as a beacon for parents and their children but also challenge and change the narratives around autism and employment, highlighting the valuable contributions that autistic individuals can make to the workforce and society.

Independent Living: Skills and Support Systems

Navigating the transition to independent living can feel like mapping a vast, uncharted territory for your young adult and you as a parent. It's about more than just finding a place to live; it's about crafting a lifestyle that supports autonomy while ensuring safety and community engagement. Let's explore the essential daily living skills your child will need, the variety of housing options available, how technology can assist in independence, and the importance of maintaining a robust support network.

Daily Living Skills

One of the most empowering sets of skills you can teach your child revolves around daily living. These skills are the bedrock of independence, encompassing everything from cooking and budgeting to personal hygiene. Each skill set can be approached gradually, celebrating each small achievement to build confidence and competence. Start with cooking, for instance, by introducing simple, safe recipes that encourage your child to explore culinary tasks, from preparing ingredients to operating kitchen appliances under supervision. Over time, as their confidence grows, more complex recipes can be introduced, always emphasizing safety and enjoyment.

Budgeting and banking are equally crucial. Begin with basic concepts like saving versus spending, want versus need, and recognizing currency values. Practical exercises, such as managing a small weekly budget for personal expenses, can demystify financial concepts. Use visual aids, like budgeting apps or charts, to make tracking income and expenses clear and engaging. For personal hygiene, structured routines help establish good habits. Use step-by-step guides or visual schedules for tasks like bathing, teeth brushing, and grooming, and consider adaptive tools designed for easier use by individuals with motor difficulties or sensory sensitivities.

Housing Options

Choosing the right living environment is pivotal in your child's successful transition to adulthood. The spectrum of housing options ranges from fully independent living, where your child may live alone or with roommates, to supported living environments that offer varying degrees of assistance. Independent living might be suitable for individuals who can manage daily tasks with minimal support, but it also requires a safety net of easily accessible community services or family support. On the other hand, supported living environments, such as group homes or residential communities specifically designed for individuals with disabilities, provide structured support that can include meal preparation, transportation, and personal care assistance.

Each option has merits and considerations, and the choice largely depends on your child's needs, abilities, and preferences. Involve your child in this decision-making process. Discuss each option's pros and cons, and if possible, visit different living arrangements together to gauge what feels most comfortable and supportive for them. This decision is not just about meeting their basic needs but about fostering a setting where they can thrive, form relationships, and engage with the community.

Maintaining a Support Network

The role of a supportive community network cannot be overstated in its impact on your child's quality of life and ongoing development. As children grow into adults, the nature of this network might evolve, but its foundation remains rooted in connections with family, friends, mentors, and professionals. Encourage your child to participate in social groups, clubs, or activities that align with their interests. These can be valuable opportunities to form friendships and improve social skills. Additionally, maintaining connections with mentors, whether teachers, therapists, or counselors, can provide guidance and encouragement as your child navigates the complexities of adult life.

Professional support services play a critical role, especially during transition or stress. Regular check-ins with healthcare providers, therapists, or adult service coordinators can help manage health needs, monitor progress in various life skills, and adjust support. Technology, too, can enhance this network. Online forums, social media groups, or virtual meet-ups can offer a sense of community and belonging, even when physical meetings are impossible.

Use of Technology for Independence

In our digital age, technology offers incredible tools to support independent living. Apps that provide reminders for medication, appointments, or daily tasks can help manage time and responsibilities efficiently. Budgeting tools and apps simplify financial management, making it accessible and understandable. For personal safety, GPS trackers and emergency alert systems can ensure that help is always within reach if needed.

Moreover, self-care apps that guide meditation, exercise, or relaxation can significantly manage stress and promote mental health. Choose apps with user-friendly interfaces and customizable features to match your child's preferences and abilities. Integrate these technologies gradually, ensuring each tool or app is a comfortable and empowering addition to their routine.

As you explore these avenues for independence, remember that each step forward is shaped by your child's unique needs, their courage to embrace new experiences, and your unwavering support as they do.

Legal Considerations: Guardianship and Beyond

Navigating the legal landscape as your child transitions into adulthood can feel like deciphering a complex map with multiple routes and important decisions at every turn. Understanding the various legal options available, such as guardianship, conservatorship, and power of attorney, is crucial in ensuring your child's rights and well-being are protected as they enter adulthood.

Different states have diverse laws affecting these decisions, so it's vital to check specific state laws to understand the options and obligations in your area. Guardianship might be necessary if your child needs help making decisions regarding health, living arrangements, or finances. In contrast, a power of attorney may be appropriate for making specific decisions on their behalf, offering a less restrictive alternative to guardianship.

Teaching self-advocacy skills to your child is more than just empowering—it's essential. As they mature, understanding their rights and learning how to express their needs effectively are invaluable skills that will serve them throughout adulthood. Start these lessons early, integrating self-advocacy into daily conversations and decisions. This might involve role-playing scenarios where they practice asking for help or expressing a preference in a safe, supportive environment. Over time, these practices can help build the confidence and skills necessary for your child to advocate for themselves in more complex situations, such as in employment or healthcare settings.

Financial security is a significant concern for many parents, and rightly so. Planning for the future is not just about setting up savings accounts; it involves understanding and navigating government benefits like Social Security, setting up special needs trusts, and ensuring your child's financial future is secure. Special needs trusts, in particular, are designed to provide for your child's extra living costs without jeopardizing their eligibility for public assistance benefits. Financial planning in this context requires specialized knowledge, so consider consulting with financial planners with special needs planning experience. They can offer guidance tailored to your family's specific situation, helping you set up a financial plan that ensures your child's needs are met now and in the future.

When it comes to legal resources and support, many organizations and groups specialize in assisting families of autistic individuals. These resources can be invaluable in helping you navigate the legal aspects of guardianship, financial planning, and rights advocacy. Organizations such as the National Disability Rights Network offer legal support and can guide you through securing the rights and services your child is entitled to. Additionally, local autism advocacy groups often have resources or can connect you with legal advisors who understand the unique needs of autistic adults. These resources can provide you with the knowledge and support necessary to make informed decisions about your child's legal and financial future, ensuring they have the protection and stability they need as they navigate adulthood.

Continuing the Journey: Maintaining Hope and Building Futures

As your child matures into adulthood, the emphasis on growth and learning continues to be a light that guides their journey. Embracing lifelong learning enriches their intellect and empowers them to navigate the complexities of the adult world with confidence and curiosity. Various educational avenues, such as adult education classes, specialized workshops, or online courses, offer platforms for continuous learning. These resources are invaluable for keeping your child engaged and intellectually stimulated. For instance, community colleges often provide a range of classes that might pique their interest, from computer programming to creative arts. Workshops can provide more focused learning opportunities, especially in life skills or specific job training. Online learning platforms offer the flexibility to learn at their own pace, which is particularly beneficial for autistic adults who may prefer a self-directed approach. Encourage your child to explore subjects that fascinate them, and support them in pursuing certifications or courses that can help further their careers or personal interests.

Maintaining physical and mental health is crucial as it significantly impacts quality of life. Encourage routines that incorporate physical activity, which is essential not only for physical health but also for mental well-being. Fitness programs tailored to their interests and abilities can make exercise an enjoyable part of their daily routine. Mental health support is equally important; ongoing therapy or counseling can provide them with strategies to manage stress, anxiety, or other emotional challenges.

Engagement in community activities can profoundly impact your child's social life and emotional well-being. Whether participating in a local art class, joining a book club, or volunteering at an animal shelter, these activities provide valuable opportunities for social interaction and community involvement. They foster a sense of belonging and can be a great source of joy and satisfaction. Encourage your child to explore different groups and activities to find what they enjoy most. Support them in joining these groups and celebrating their courage in stepping out into the community. This engagement is a stepping stone to building a supportive social network that nurtures their emotional health and enriches their life experiences.

Celebrating milestones and achievements in adolescence and adulthood is as vital as it was during childhood. These celebrations affirm your child's growth and accomplishments, whether related to personal goals, educational achievements, or career advancements. Celebrate these milestones with enthusiasm and pride. Whether it's a job promotion, moving into their apartment, or mastering a new skill, each achievement is a testament to their persistence and hard work. These celebrations reinforce the message of hope and ongoing development, reminding your child that every effort is meaningful and every achievement is worth honoring.

In essence, the transition into adulthood extends the growth and learning that has marked your child's life. It is a phase filled with opportunities for further education, deeper community involvement, and significant personal growth. By supporting their continuous learning, encouraging active participation in the community, and celebrating their achievements, you empower your child to lead a fulfilling, enriched life. This ongoing support and recognition of their efforts foster hope and confidence, ensuring they feel valued and understood as they navigate adulthood.

Final Words

As we end our time together, I want to take a moment to reflect on the profound journey of raising an autistic child. From those initial, often overwhelming days following diagnosis through the evolving challenges of growth and learning to the broader horizon of adulthood, your path is marked by resilience and transformation. Together, we've explored how integrating traditional approaches with holistic methods—like mindfulness, creative expression, and self-awareness—can enrich your family's experience and give your child a robust foundation for success.

In every chapter, we've emphasized a strength-based perspective as crucial to recognizing and celebrating the unique strengths and potential of our autistic children. Seeing beyond the challenges to acknowledge and foster these strengths can lead to more fulfilling outcomes and a richer understanding of your child's capabilities. This approach doesn't just support their growth; it transforms how we think about potential and success.

Balancing this drive for growth with self-compassion is vital. It reminds us to honor our limits and those of our children. Parenting is a demanding journey, and it's okay to acknowledge that you're doing your best in a challenging role. Allow yourself the grace to accept where you are, knowing each step is part of a larger journey toward growth and understanding.

I urge you to continue learning and advocating for your child. Stay engaged with the latest research and resources available in the autism community. Your proactive efforts make a significant difference in navigating the educational, social, and medical landscapes that impact your child's life.

Also, let me reaffirm that you are not alone. A vibrant community of parents, educators, and professionals is on this journey with you, each with their own stories of challenges and triumphs. This community is a source of support, inspiration, and understanding. I encourage you to lean on, contribute, and grow with it.

Envision a future where your child leads a fulfilling life, empowered by their unique desires, perspectives, and talents. This vision is not just a dream; it's a possibility that you are helping to shape with your dedication and love. Your efforts pave the way for a society that values and embraces neurodiversity, recognizing it as a vital and enriching aspect of the human experience.

In closing, thank you for your commitment and courage. Thank you for opening your heart and mind to the strategies and perspectives shared in this book. Your willingness to embrace this journey shapes your child's life and contributes to broader societal shifts toward acceptance and inclusion.

Together, let's continue to advocate for a world that appreciates and celebrates the diverse spectrum of the human brain. Here's to the ongoing journey, the shared experiences, and the collective hope for a future where everyone is valued for who they are.

Final Words

Paying it Forward to Another Parent

Alone, we can do so little; together, we can do so much.

— Helen Keller

If you've gained valuable insights and tools to support your child and family by reading *The Art and Science of Raising Your Autistic Child,* it's time to pay it forward.

Sharing your experience can help other parents and caregivers find the guidance they need—just as you did.

Your honest review on the platform where you purchased this book is invaluable. It can guide someone else on their journey, offering them the support and hope they seek.

Your review is not just a review; it's a beacon of hope for someone else on their own path. Your words can be the guiding light that leads them to the support and understanding they need.

With gratitude,

K.M. Burnham

Appendix of Support Therapies

This alphabetical list provides a guide to many (but not all) of the types of therapies available to autistic children. It has been put together from the references used throughout the book. Because new evidence-based therapies are constantly being designed, consulting with trained and qualified professionals is critical to determine the most effective therapies for your child and ensure they are appropriately implemented.

Applied Behavior Analysis (ABA)

Description: A structured approach that uses reinforcement strategies to teach social, communication, and learning skills.

Benefits: Proven effectiveness in increasing communication, social skills, and learning; improves daily functioning.

Cautions: The intensity, rigidity, and lack of individualization of the programs can be **very stressful** for many children, making this type of therapy fall out of favor in the community.

ACUPUNCTURE/ACUPRESSURE

DESCRIPTION: Traditional Chinese medicine technique uses thin needles inserted/or hands to apply pressure to specific points on the body to balance energy flow.

BENEFITS: May reduce anxiety and stress, improve mood, and aid pain management.

CAUTIONS: Must be performed by a licensed practitioner; effectiveness varies, and scientific support is limited but increasing.

ANIMAL-ASSISTED THERAPY

DESCRIPTION: Involves interactions with animals (e.g., dogs, horses) to promote social interaction, reduce anxiety, and improve mood.

BENEFITS: Enhances social interactions, reduces stress and anxiety, and promotes joy.

CAUTIONS: Consider allergies and phobias; ensure animals are well-trained and safe.

ART THERAPY

DESCRIPTION: Uses creative arts (drawing, painting, sculpting) to express emotions, improve sensory processing, and enhance social skills.

BENEFITS: Enhances emotional expression, reduces anxiety, improves fine motor skills, and fosters creativity.

CAUTIONS: Should be guided by a trained therapist to avoid frustration or sensory overload.

COGNITIVE BEHAVIORAL THERAPY (CBT)

DESCRIPTION: Helps individuals manage emotions and behaviors by changing negative thought patterns.

BENEFITS: Effective in reducing anxiety, managing behaviors, and improving emotional regulation.

CAUTIONS: Requires cognitive abilities to understand and apply concepts; may not be suitable for all.

CRANIOSACRAL THERAPY

DESCRIPTION: A gentle, hands-on approach to release tension in the central nervous system to improve overall body function.

BENEFITS: May reduce stress and tension, promote relaxation, and potentially enhance physical functioning.

CAUTIONS: Lack of extensive scientific evidence; should be used as a complementary therapy.

DANCE/MOVEMENT THERAPY

DESCRIPTION: Uses movement and dance to improve emotional expression, social interaction, and body awareness.

BENEFITS: Improves motor skills, enhances emotional expression, and fosters social interaction.

CAUTIONS: Ensure activities are suited to the individual's physical abilities to avoid injury.

DIETARY AND NUTRITIONAL INTERVENTIONS

DESCRIPTION: Focuses on special diets (e.g., gluten-free, casein-free) and supplements to address potential food sensitivities and nutritional deficiencies.

BENEFITS: Can improve gastrointestinal health, reduce distress symptoms, and potentially positively impact behavior.

CAUTIONS: Should be supervised by a healthcare provider to ensure nutritional balance and avoid potential adverse effects.

FLOORTIME (ALSO KNOWN AS DIRFloortime®)

DESCRIPTION: Encourages emotional and developmental growth through play and relationship-building activities.

BENEFITS: Supports emotional development, enhances creativity, and improves interactions.

CAUTIONS: Requires active participation from caregivers and can be time-consuming.

MINDFULNESS AND MEDITATION

DESCRIPTION: Techniques like deep breathing, guided imagery, and body scans to improve self-regulation, reduce stress, and enhance focus.

BENEFITS: Promotes calmness, enhances focus, improves emotional regulation, and expands body awareness.

CAUTIONS: Work with a trained professional and start with short sessions to prevent frustration or anxiety.

MUSIC THERAPY:

DESCRIPTION: Utilizes music activities (e.g., playing instruments, singing, listening) to improve communication, social skills, and emotional regulation.

BENEFITS: Aids in emotional expression, enhances auditory processing, and can improve verbal and nonverbal communication.

CAUTIONS: Must be personalized to avoid overstimulation or anxiety.

OCCUPATIONAL THERAPY (OT)

DESCRIPTION: Helps improve daily living skills, motor skills, and sensory processing abilities.

BENEFITS: Enhances independence in daily activities, improves motor skills, and helps with sensory integration.

CAUTIONS: To avoid frustration, it should be tailored to the individual's specific needs and administered by a trained occupational therapist.

PHYSICAL THERAPY (PT)

DESCRIPTION: Addresses physical and motor skills to improve mobility, coordination, and physical health.

BENEFITS: Improves physical health, enhances motor skills, and increases coordination.

CAUTIONS: Activities should be appropriate for the individual's physical capabilities to prevent injury.

Appendix of Support Therapies

Relationship Development Intervention (RDI)

Description: Focuses on developing emotional and social connections through guided participation and activities.

Benefits: Promotes emotional and social growth, enhances communication, and strengthens family relationships.

Cautions: Time-intensive; requires active parental involvement and trained professionals.

Sensory Integration Therapy:

Description: Involves activities to help individuals process and respond to sensory information more effectively.

Benefits: Improves sensory processing, enhances coordination, and helps in daily functioning.

Cautions: Should be conducted by an occupational therapist trained in sensory integration techniques.

Social Skills Training

Description: Teaches skills for interacting with peers, understanding social cues, and building relationships.

Benefits: Enhances social understanding and peer relationships, improves communication, and fosters community involvement.

Cautions: Needs to be contextually relevant and practiced in natural settings to be effective.

Speech Therapy

Description: Focuses on improving communication skills, including speech, language, and nonverbal communication.

Benefits: Improves verbal skills, enhances nonverbal communication, and aids social communication.

Cautions: Requires consistent practice; should be delivered by a licensed speech-language pathologist.

Yoga (adaptive):

Description: Combines physical postures, breathing exercises, and meditation to improve body awareness, reduce anxiety, and enhance focus.

Benefits: Increases body awareness, improves flexibility and strength, and aids in stress management.

Cautions: Should be adapted to individual abilities and needs to prevent physical strain.

References

CHAPTER 1

Balasco, L., Provenzano, G., & Bozzi, Y. (2020). Sensory abnormalities in autism spectrum disorders: A focus on the tactile domain, from genetic mouse models to the clinic. *Frontiers in Psychiatry, 10*, 464344. https://doi.org/10.3389/fpsyt.2019.01016

Bellone, K. M., Elliott, S. C., Hynan, L. S., Warren, B., & Jarrett, R. B. (2023). Mindful self-care for caregivers: A proof of concept study investigating a model for embedded caregiver support in a pediatric setting. *Journal of Autism and Developmental Disorders, 53*(2), 539-552. https://doi.org/10.1007/s10803-021-05113-6

Bohadana, G., Morrissey, S., & Paynter, J. (2019). Self-compassion: A novel predictor of stress and quality of life in parents of children with autism spectrum disorder. *Journal of Autism and Developmental Disorders, 49*(10), 4039-4052. https://doi.org/10.1007/s10803-019-04121-x

Dunia, G., Carballo, G., & Garcia-Retamero, R. (2020). Siblings of children with autism spectrum disorders: social support and family quality of life. *Quality of Life Research, 29*(5), 1193-1202. https://doi.org/10.1007/s11136-020-02429-1

Krishnan, R., Russell, P. S. S., & Russell, S. (2017). A focus group study to explore grief experiences among parents of children with autism spectrum disorder. *Journal of the Indian Academy of Applied Psychology, 43*(2), 267-275. https://www.proquest.com/scholarly-journals/focus-group-study-explore-grief-experiences-among/docview/1964553501/se-2

Lunsky, Y., Fung, K., Lake, J. et al. (2018). Evaluation of Acceptance and Commitment Therapy (ACT) for mothers of children and youth with autism spectrum disorder. *Mindfulness 9*, 1110–1116. https://doi.org/10.1007/s12671-017-0846-3

Oshima, F., Takahashi, T., Tamura, M., Guan, S., Seto, M., Hull, L., Mandy, W., Tsuchiya, K., & Shimizu, E. (2024). The association between social camouflage and mental health among autistic people in Japan and the UK: a cross-cultural study. *Molecular Autism, 15*, 1-13. https://doi.org/10.1186/s13229-023-00579-w

References

Schuck, R. K., Tagavi, D. M., Baiden, K. M. P., Dwyer, P., Williams, Z. J., Osuna, A., Ferguson, E. F., Jimenez Muñoz, M., Poyser, S. K., Johnson, J. F., & Vernon, T. W. (2022). Neurodiversity and autism intervention: Reconciling perspectives through a naturalistic developmental behavioral intervention framework. *Journal of Autism and Developmental Disorders, 52*(10), 4625-4645. https://doi.org/10.1007/s10803-021-05316-x

Thomas, S., Barnett, L. M., Papadopoulos, N., Lander, N., McGillivray, J., & Rinehart, N. (2022). How do physical activity and sedentary behaviour affect motor competence in children with autism spectrum disorder compared to typically developing children: A pilot study. *Journal of Autism and Developmental Disorders, 52*(8), 3443-3455. https://doi.org/10.1007/s10803-021-05205-3

Wright, B. M., & Benigno, J. P. (2019). Autism spectrum disorder and sibling relationships: Exploring implications for intervention using a family systems framework. *American Journal of Speech - Language Pathology (Online), 28*(2), 759-767. https://doi.org/10.1044/2018AJSLP-18-0088

CHAPTER 2

Aftab, A., Sehgal, C. A., Noohu, M. M., & Jaleel, G. (2023). Clinical effectiveness of aac intervention in minimally verbal children with asd: A systematic review. *NeuroRegulation, 10*(4), 239-252. https://doi.org/10.15540/nr.10.4.239

Leonet, O., Orcasitas-Vicandi, M., Langarika-Rocafort, A., Mondragon, N. I., & Etxebarrieta, G. R. (2022). A systematic review of augmentative and alternative communication interventions for children aged from 0 to 6 years. *Language, Speech & Hearing Services in Schools (Online), 53*(3), 894-920. 10.m44/2022LSHSS-21-00191

PECUSA.com. (2023, April 17). PECS®: An evidence-based practice -. Pyramid Educational Consultants. https://pecsusa.com/pecs/

Schuck, R. K., Tagavi, D. M., Baiden, K. M. P., Dwyer, P., Williams, Z. J., Osuna, A., Ferguson, E. F., Jimenez Muñoz, M., Poyser, S. K., Johnson, J. F., & Vernon, T. W. (2022). Neurodiversity and autism intervention: Reconciling perspectives through a naturalistic developmental behavioral intervention framework. *Journal of Autism and Developmental Disorders, 52*(10), 4625-4645. https://doi.org/10.1007/s10803-021-05316-x

References

Swanson, M. R. (2020). The role of caregiver speech in supporting language development in infants and toddlers with autism spectrum disorder. *Development and Psychopathology, 32*(4), 1230-1239. https://doi.org/10.1017/S0954579420000838

CHAPTER 3

Autism Research Institute. (2024, July 17). Meltdowns & calming techniques in autism. https://autism.org/meltdowns-calming-techniques-in-autism/

Bellone, K. M., Elliott, S. C., Hynan, L. S., Warren, B., & Jarrett, R. B. (2023). Mindful self-care for caregivers: A proof of concept study investigating a model for embedded caregiver support in a pediatric setting. *Journal of Autism and Developmental Disorders, 53*(2), 539-552. https://doi.org/10.1007/s10803-021-05113-6

Bohadana, G., Morrissey, S., & Paynter, J. (2019). Self-compassion: A novel predictor of stress and quality of life in parents of children with autism spectrum disorder. *Journal of Autism and Developmental Disorders, 49*(10), 4039-4052. https://doi.org/10.1007/s10803-019-04121-x

Chou, Y. (2023). Escape from emotional distress: A curriculum model to enhance self-directed emotion regulation of students with autism spectrum disorder. *Education and Training in Autism and Developmental Disabilities, 58*(1), 106-122. https://www.proquest.com/scholarly-journals/escape-emotional-distress-curriculum-model/docview/2777274797/se-2

Lunsky, Y., Fung, K., Lake, J. et al. Evaluation of acceptance and commitment therapy (act) for mothers of children and youth with autism spectrum disorder. *Mindfulness 9,* 1110–1116 (2018). https://doi.org/10.1007/s12671-017-0846-3

Schuck, R. K., Tagavi, D. M., Baiden, K. M. P., Dwyer, P., Williams, Z. J., Osuna, A., Ferguson, E. F., Jimenez Muñoz, M., Poyser, S. K., Johnson, J. F., & Vernon, T. W. (2022). Neurodiversity and autism intervention: Reconciling perspectives through a naturalistic developmental behavioral intervention framework. *Journal of Autism and Developmental Disorders, 52*(10), 4625-4645. https://doi.org/10.1007/s10803-021-05316-x

CHAPTER 4

Best Buddies International. (2024, April 26). Why We Matter. https://www.bestbuddies.org/what-we-do/mission-vision-goals/

Chester, M., Richdale, A. L., & McGillivray, J. (2019). Group-based social skills training with play for children on the autism spectrum. *Journal of Autism and Developmental Disorders, 49*(6), 2231-2242. https://doi.org/10.1007/s10803-019-03892-7

References

Fridenson-hayo, S., Berggren, S., Lassalle, A., Tal, S., Pigat, D., Meir-goren, N., O'reilly, H., Ben-zur, S., Bölte, S., Baron-cohen, S., & Golan, O. (2017). 'Emotiplay': a serious game for learning about emotions in children with autism: results of a cross-cultural evaluation. *European Child & Adolescent Psychiatry, 26*(8), 979-992. https://doi.org/10.1007/s00787-017-0968-0

Radley, K. C., Ford, W. B., Mchugh, M. B., Dadakhodjaeva, K., O'handley, R.,D., Battaglia, A. A., Lum, J. D., & K. (2015). Brief report: Use of superheroes social skills to promote accurate social skill use in children with autism spectrum disorder. *Journal of Autism and Developmental Disorders, 45*(9), 3048-3054. https://doi.org/10.1007/s10803-015-2442-5

Schuck, R. K., Tagavi, D. M., Baiden, K. M. P., Dwyer, P., Williams, Z. J., Osuna, A., Ferguson, E. F., Jimenez Muñoz, M., Poyser, S. K., Johnson, J. F., & Vernon, T. W. (2022). Neurodiversity and autism intervention: Reconciling perspectives through a naturalistic developmental behavioral intervention framework. *Journal of Autism and Developmental Disorders, 52*(10), 4625-4645. https://doi.org/10.1007/s10803-021-05316-x

Thomas, S., Barnett, L. M., Papadopoulos, N., Lander, N., McGillivray, J., & Rinehart, N. (2022). How do physical activity and sedentary behaviour affect motor competence in children with autism spectrum disorder compared to typically developing children: A pilot study. *Journal of Autism and Developmental Disorders, 52*(8), 3443-3455. https://doi.org/10.1007/s10803-021-05205-3

CHAPTER 5

Attfield, K. (2022). The "feeling-life" journey of the grade school child: An investigation into inclusive young citizenship in international Waldorf education. *Journal of Curriculum and Pedagogy, 20*(4), 276–299. https://doi.org/10.1080/15505170.2022.2034682

Fadare, M. C. M., Carrera, B. B., Fadare, S. A., & Paguia, D. B. (2021). Parents' challenges of home-schooling children with autism spectrum disorder: A special journey. *International Journal of Science and Management Studies (IJSMS), 4*(4), 11-26.

Laura, F., Jalisa, G., Beaudoin, E., & Sladeczek, I. E. (2020). Barriers to and facilitators of successful early school transitions for children with autism spectrum disorders and other developmental disabilities: A systematic review. *Journal of Autism and Developmental Disorders, 50*(6), 1866-1881. https://doi.org/10.1007/s10803-019-03938-w

References

Leifler, E., Carpelan, G., Zakrevska, A., Bölte, S., & Jonsson, U. (2020). Does the learning environment 'make the grade'? A systematic review of accommodations for children on the autism spectrum in mainstream school. *Scandinavian Journal of Occupational Therapy, 28*(8), 582–597. https://doi.org/10.1080/11038128.2020.1832145

U.S. Department of Education. (2024, July 24). Individuals with disabilities education act (IDEA). Individuals with Disabilities Education Act. https://sites.ed.gov/idea/

U.S. Department of Justice. (n.d.). The Americans with disabilities act. ADA.gov. https://www.ada.gov/

Vasiļonoks, A., Zīle, I., & Folkmanis, V. (2018). Efficiency of multisensoric therapy in autism spectrum disorder patients. *Proceedings of the Latvian Academy of Sciences, 72*(3), 193-195. https://doi.org/10.2478/prolas-2018-0022

Kidd, T., & Kaczmarek, E. (2010). The experiences of mothers home educating their children with autism spectrum disorder. *Issues in Educational Research, 20*(3), 257-275. https://www.proquest.com/scholarly-journals/experiences-mothers-home-educating-their-children/docview/2393183075/se-2

CHAPTER 6

Hangül, Z., & Tufan, A. E. (2022). Use of complementary and alternative therapies in autism spectrum disorder. *Current Approaches in Psychology, 14*(2), 165-173. https://doi.org/10.18863/pgy.935207

Hartley, M., Dorstyn, D., & Due, C. (2019). Mindfulness for Children and Adults with Autism Spectrum Disorder and Their Caregivers: A Meta-analysis. *Journal of Autism and Developmental Disorders, 49*(10), 4306-4319. https://doi.org/10.1007/s10803-019-04145-3

The International Council on Development and Learning, Inc. (n.d.). What is floortime?. Home of DIRFloortime® (Floortime). https://www.icdl.com/floortime

Ju, X., Liu, H., Xu, J., Hu, B., Jin, Y., & Chang, L. (2024). Effect of Yoga Intervention on Problem Behavior and Motor Coordination in Children with Autism. *Behavioral Sciences, 14*(2), 116. https://doi.org/10.3390/bs14020116

LaGasse, A. B. (2014). Effects of a Music Therapy Group Intervention on Enhancing Social Skills in Children with Autism. *Journal of Music Therapy, 51*(3), 250-75. https://www.proquest.com/scholarly-journals/effects-music-therapy-group-intervention-on/docview/1627710689/se-2

References

Oligbo, M., Lawson, L. M., & Vaduvathiriyan, P. (2023). Motor interventions for children with autism spectrum disorder: A scoping review. *Therapeutic Recreation Journal, 57*(4), 340-364. https://doi.org/10.18666/TRJ-2023-V57-I4-11995

Schuck, R. K., Tagavi, D. M., Baiden, K. M. P., Dwyer, P., Williams, Z. J., Osuna, A., Ferguson, E. F., Jimenez Muñoz, M., Poyser, S. K., Johnson, J. F., & Vernon, T. W. (2022). Neurodiversity and autism intervention: Reconciling perspectives through a naturalistic developmental behavioral intervention framework. *Journal of Autism and Developmental Disorders, 52*(10), 4625-4645. https://doi.org/10.1007/s10803-021-05316-x

Susanu, N. (2019). Art-therapy - Cognitive-behavioral approach art-therapy method of working with children with T.S.A. *New Trends in Psychology, 1*(2) https://www.proquest.com/scholarly-journals/art-therapy-cognitive-behavioral-approach-method/docview/2585933845/se-2

Thomas, S., Barnett, L. M., Papadopoulos, N., Lander, N., McGillivray, J., & Rinehart, N. (2022). How do physical activity and sedentary behaviour affect motor competence in children with autism spectrum disorder compared to typically developing children: A pilot study. *Journal of Autism and Developmental Disorders, 52*(8), 3443-3455. https://doi.org/10.1007/s10803-021-05205-3

Chapter 7

Autistic Self Advocacy Network. (2024, July 31). Autistic Self Advocacy Network. https://autisticadvocacy.org/

Bellone, K. M., Elliott, S. C., Hynan, L. S., Warren, B., & Jarrett, R. B. (2023). Mindful self-care for caregivers: A proof of concept study investigating a model for embedded caregiver support in a pediatric setting. *Journal of Autism and Developmental Disorders, 53*(2), 539-552. https://doi.org/10.1007/s10803-021-05113-6

Bohadana, G., Morrissey, S., & Paynter, J. (2019). Self-compassion: A novel predictor of stress and quality of life in parents of children with autism spectrum disorder. *Journal of Autism and Developmental Disorders, 49*(10), 4039-4052. https://doi.org/10.1007/s10803-019-04121-x

Delgado, E. B., Wenceslao Peñate Castro, & Alicia Díaz Megolla. (2024). Relationship between parenting educational styles and well-being in families with autistic children: A systematic review. *European Journal of Investigation in Health, Psychology and Education, 14*(6), 1527. https://doi.org/10.3390/ejihpe14060101

References

Dunia, G., Carballo, G., & Garcia-Retamero, R. (2020). Siblings of children with autism spectrum disorders: social support and family quality of life. *Quality of Life Research, 29*(5), 1193-1202. https://doi.org/10.1007/s11136-020-02429-1

Ren, X., Cai, Y., Wang, J., & Chen, O. (2024). A systematic review of parental burnout and related factors among parents. *BMC Public Health, 24*, 1-17. https://doi.org/10.1186/s12889-024-17829-y

Tawwab, N. G. (2021). Set boundaries, find peace: A guide to reclaiming yourself. TarcherPerigee, an imprint of Penguin Random House LLC.

Wolff, B., Magiati, I., Roberts, R., Skoss, R., & Glasson, E. J. (2023). Psychosocial interventions and support groups for siblings of individuals with neurodevelopmental conditions: A mixed methods systematic review of sibling self-reported mental health and wellbeing outcomes. *Clinical Child and Family Psychology Review, 26*(1), 143-189. https://doi.org/10.1007/s10567-022-00413-4

Wright, B. M., & Benigno, J. P. (2019). Autism spectrum disorder and sibling relationships: Exploring implications for intervention using a family systems framework. *American Journal of Speech - Language Pathology (Online), 28*(2), 759-767. https://doi.org/10.1044/2018AJSLP-18-0088

CHAPTER 8

Autistic Self Advocacy Network. (2024, July 31). Autistic Self Advocacy Network. https://autisticadvocacy.org/

Currin, C. (2023, October 4). Financial planning 101: Providing for an autistic child. Organization for Autism Research. https://researchautism.org/oaracle-newsletter/financial-planning-101-providing-for-an-autistic-child/

Hantman, R.M., Johnston, E.B. & Tager-Flusberg, H. Parental perspectives: How sensory sensitivities impact the transition to adulthood in adolescents and young adults with autism spectrum disorder. *Journal of Autism and Developmental Disorders 54*, 544–562 (2024). https://doi.org/10.1007/s10803-022-05815-5

Laura, F., Jalisa, G., Beaudoin, E., & Sladeczek, I. E. (2020). Barriers to and facilitators of successful early school transitions for children with autism spectrum disorders and other developmental disabilities: A systematic review. *Journal of Autism and Developmental Disorders, 50*(6), 1866-1881. https://doi.org/10.1007/s10803-019-03938-w

Leaf, J. B., Cihon, J. H., Ferguson, J. L., & Gerhardt, P. F. (Eds.). (2022). Handbook of quality of life for individuals with autism spectrum disorder. Springer International Publishing AG.

References

National Disability Rights Network. (2024, June 17).NDRN. https://www. ndrn.org/

U.S. Department of Justice. (n.d.). The Americans with disabilities act. ADA.gov. https://www.ada.gov/

Acknowledgments

I want to express my deep appreciation to the incredible families who shared their stories and experiences for this book. To protect their privacy, names and other identifiable details have been changed. Your loving commitment to your children makes a difference in their world, which is also ours. I also want to thank my family and friends for their unwavering support and encouragement throughout this journey, not just the journey of this book but also the journey of raising my daughters. Your compassion and supportive actions have made all the difference in my life and my ability to see this project through.

About the Author

K.M. Burnham is a passionate advocate for neurodiversity and a devoted mother of two autistic adults. Drawing from her personal experiences, she has dedicated her career to creating inclusive environments that celebrate individuality and promote understanding. As a late-diagnosed neurodivergent individual, K.M. brings a deeply personal perspective to her writing. She aims to provide evidence-based resources that are accessible and relatable, helping people thrive in their unique journeys. Her mission is to create a world where every voice is heard, and every experience is valued, fostering a culture of equity and compassion. When she's not writing, speaking, or advocating for neurodiverse-affirming practices in parenting and leadership, K.M. enjoys spending quality time outdoors, playing games with her family and friends, knitting, and painting in watercolor.

www.ingramcontent.com/pod-product-compliance
Lightning Source LLC
Chambersburg PA
CBHW070709130626
46553CB00005B/1914